IMAGES OF W

ARMOURED WARFARE

IN THE NORTH AFRICAN CAMPAIGN

CW00409254

Frontispiece: An M3 Grant medium tank in North Africa. (*US Army/NARA*)

IMAGES OF WAR

ARMOURED WARFARE

IN THE NORTH AFRICAN CAMPAIGN

RARE PHOTOGRAPHS FROM
WARTIME ARCHIVES

ANTHONY TUCKER-JONES

Pen & Sword
MILITARY

First published in Great Britain in 2011 by
PEN & SWORD MILITARY
an imprint of
Pen & Sword Books Ltd,
47 Church Street,
Barnsley,
South Yorkshire.
S70 2AS

Copyright © Anthony Tucker-Jones, 2011

A CIP record for this book is available from the British Library.

ISBN 978184 884 5671

The right of Anthony Tucker-Jones to be identified as Author of this Work
has been asserted by him in accordance with the Copyright, Designs and
Patents Act 1988.

All rights reserved. No part of this book may be reproduced or
transmitted in any form or by any means, electronic or mechanical
including photocopying, recording or by any information storage and
retrieval system, without permission from the Publisher in writing.

Typeset by Chic Media Ltd

Printed and bound by CPI

Pen & Sword Books Ltd incorporates the Imprints of
Pen & Sword Aviation, Pen & Sword Family History, Pen & Sword
Maritime, Pen & Sword Military, Pen & Sword Discovery, Wharncliffe Local
History, Wharncliffe True Crime, Wharncliffe Transport, Pen & Sword
Select, Pen & Sword Military Classics, Leo Cooper, The Praetorian Press,
Remember When, Seaforth Publishing and Frontline Publishing.

For a complete list of Pen & Sword titles please contact
Pen & Sword Books Limited
47 Church Street, Barnsley, South Yorkshire, S70 2AS, England
E-mail: enquiries@pen-and-sword.co.uk
Website: www.pen-and-sword.co.uk

Contents

Introduction

The battles fought in North Africa during the Second World War are largely remembered for the exploits of Field Marshal Erwin Rommel, the 'Desert Fox', and the British 7th Armoured Division, the 'Desert Rats.' Field Marshal Bernard Montgomery also established his reputation there with the decisive victory at El Alamein that sealed Rommel's fate.

The highly mobile armoured warfare in North Africa was essentially a clean war, a soldier's war. The open desert wastes in Egypt and Libya were ideal for tanks, with few towns and civilians to distract from the business of fighting (or, indeed, result in atrocities). When the fighting moved into Tunisia, the landscape changed, with the Axis forces taking to the mountains. North Africa's geography and climate meant that the style of mechanised warfare fought there was very different from that in France, Italy and Russia.

The vast Western Desert stretches almost 400 miles from El Alamein in Egypt to Gazala in Libya. Some 150 miles to the south are the Jarabub and Siwa oases, while north of the coastal road lies the shore of the Mediterranean Sea. Along the coast of Libya's Cyrenaica province are Bardia and Tobruk, then the coastal bulge at Djebel Akhdar with the towns of Derna and Benghazi, and further westward Mersa Brega and El Agheila. Key choke-points are the Fuka, Halfaya and Sidi Rezegh passes. It was from Agheila to Alamein and back again that the critical battles between the Eighth Army and the German Afrika Korps took place.

The vast, open desert sands of North Africa seemed an ideal place to fight decisive tank battles, but things are rarely that simple. Both sides struggled to maintain their lengthy and dangerously exposed lines of communication; any victory inevitably meant additional supply problems for the victors, which then tilted the fortunes of war back the other way. The naval and air war in the Mediterranean also impinged on both sides' ability to deliver vital supplies and replacement equipment.

The basic tasks of moving, resupply and reconnaissance soaked up the lion's share of the time; combat was typically restricted to daylight and even then actual fighting only accounted for about three or four hours a day. British armoured and infantry units at nightfall often withdrew up to 5 miles from the scene of the action to form protective leaguers, like old-fashioned wagon trains. At rest both sides formed protective boxes with all-round covering fire for defence.

By June 1940 France was out of the war, leaving Benito Mussolini free to attack

British-controlled Egypt from his Libyan colony. With almost half a million Italian troops in Libya and in Italian East Africa, the situation in Egypt looked particularly grim. Nonetheless, while Mussolini's forces enjoyed supremacy in the air and at sea, his armoured fighting vehicles were another matter altogether. The Italian Army suffered from poor mobility and limited mechanisation, both crucial ingredients for prosecuting a successful invasion.

Although Mussolini was convinced that Britain would surrender after the fall of France, by August 1940 Winston Churchill had not succumbed to Adolf Hitler's plans for a Nazi invasion of Britain and the Italian dictator was forced to strike in Egypt. Unfortunately for the Italian soldiers, Mussolini had gained an inflated impression of his military capabilities following his invasion of Abyssinia and his intervention in the Spanish Civil War in the mid-1930s.

Hitler and other advocates of mechanised warfare had watched with interest the Italian Army's performance during both of these wars. In fact, Hitler had tried to dissuade Mussolini from his Abyssinian conquest, seeing it as an unnecessary diversion, but in 1935 Mussolini had thrown three army corps, supported by light tanks, artillery, aircraft and poison gas, against the Abyssinians. An Abyssinian counter-offensive drove Mussolini's forces back, ironically using German- and Japanese-supplied weapons. Air power was the deciding factor in Abyssinia, not tanks. In May 1936 Mussolini annexed the country and then committed himself to General Franco's Nationalist cause in Spain.

His forces first saw action during the Malaga campaign in 1937, and on this occasion nothing could stop the Italian light tanks – not least because a third of the Republican troops did not even have rifles. Mussolini was elated by the prowess of his troops. In February 1937, however, in what is generally regarded as the first armoured battle of modern times, at Guadalajara, north-east of Madrid, his light tanks proved all but useless in the face of local Republican air superiority and armour.

Mussolini's invasion of Egypt in 1940 turned out to be half-hearted, to say the least. Unfortunately Churchill missed his chance to finish off the Italian Army after the remarkable victory at Beda Fomm, as he was distracted by Mussolini's ill-conceived invasion of Greece and allowed the British momentum in North Africa to be lost. At this point Hitler stepped in, propping up his ally by dispatching to his aid the Afrika Korps under Erwin Rommel. Within two weeks Rommel had reached the Egyptian frontier, with only Tobruk holding out in his rear. The Australian defenders, however, resolutely refused to give up and for the first time the panzers found themselves driving through infantry who did not automatically surrender.

All the successes of Generals Wavell and O'Connor were swept away in a month. The *Berliner Illustrierte* ran a series called 'The Heroes of Halfaya', relating how

Rommel had thrashed the British in a three-day battle. War correspondent Alexander Clifford saw captured copies and noted: 'it was good, exciting stuff, surprisingly complimentary to the British.'

During the next two years Rommel took on a succession of British commanders, in the process perfecting his defensive-offensive method of mechanised warfare – in Rommel's parlance, first the shield, then the sword. At first, repeated British efforts to drive Rommel back from the frontier were unsuccessful, but Hitler's apparent indifference to the North African campaign until it was too late meant that Rommel found himself fighting a war of attrition that he could not win, despite his genius as an armoured fighting tactician.

The turning point finally came in October/November 1942, by which time the Axis forces were completely outnumbered in both manpower and equipment. Following the Allied landings in French North Africa, Rommel, denied the resources he needed to deliver a knock-out blow, was forced to fight a two-front war that was ultimately unwinnable.

Photograph Sources

The author is indebted to a number of individuals who were kind enough to share their private collections and offer their expertise, in particular military historian Dr Peter Caddick-Adams, author of *Monty and Rommel: Parallel Lives*, who made available his photographs of the Deutsches Afrika Korps; Steve Hunnisett and Paul Lazzell, whose fathers Ron and Bill served with the Royal Artillery, and Raine Alexander, whose father served with the Royal Army Service Corps in North Africa. Their photographs offer a very personal insight into the conduct of the war fought in the desert sands and mountains of North Africa.

Preston Isaac, Chairman of the Military Vehicle Trust and owner of the Cobbaton Combat Collection, provided Basil Lancaster's photographs taken in East Africa. Images have also been drawn from the American National Archives and Records Administration (NARA), which include the US Army and Signal Corps collections covering the North African Campaign, as well as the author's own collection built up over the last thirty years from a wide variety of sources.

Chapter One

Mussolini's Panzers

'When Mussolini declared war on Great Britain at the moment of the fall of France in 1940, the Italian Empire in North and East Africa presented a majestic appearance,' remarked British Prime Minister Winston Churchill. Although Churchill had his hands full with Hitler, who now straddled all of Europe, he knew he could not ignore the posturing Italian dictator Benito Mussolini. Churchill wrote of this threat: 'In June 1940, when the British Empire seemed to Fascist eyes reeling to ruin, and France was almost prostrate, the Italian Empire in Africa spread far and wide. Libya, Eritrea, Abyssinia [Ethiopia], Somaliland, nourished by Italian taxation, comprised a vast region in which nearly a quarter of a million Italian colonists toiled and began to thrive, under the protection of more than 400,000 Italian and native troops.'

By 1940 Mussolini considered himself the strong man of Africa. Superficially at least he was in a dominant position and General Sir Archibald Wavell, the British Commander-in-Chief Middle East, knew it. Nonetheless by no stretch of the imagination were the Italian forces mechanised in the same sense as the victorious German Wehrmacht. The Italian Army in North Africa, in what is now Libya, consisted primarily of conscripted Italian and Libyan infantry. It was a marching force, short of everything but particularly tanks, transport and artillery – essentially all the necessities of modern war. In addition, training was poor and although the morale of the few tank and artillery units was good, the calibre of their weapons was simply inadequate.

Although Mussolini had sided with Hitler in the May 1939 Pact of Steel, he knew his country would not be ready for war with the Western powers until 1941 or 1942, but Hitler would not wait. Under the Rome–Berlin Axis agreement, Hitler gained an Italian tank force, comprising three Italian armoured divisions, in the sun-baked wastes of North Africa. However, Hitler's panzer specialists had little confidence in the Italian Army's capabilities. In the early 1930s Major Nehring had been sent on an exchange with the Italian Army and examined their developing tank force. He cannot have been very impressed with the pace of development or their tactical thinking. The L3 tankette was just going into production and the Italians were still six years away from producing their first medium tank. The M11/39 prototype appeared in 1937, whereas the Panzer III and IV went into limited production that year.

Luckily for Churchill and the British Army, Mussolini's L3 tankette was not suitable for modern tank warfare and the M11/39 medium tank was poorly designed. At the first opportunity the M11/39 was replaced with the much better M13/40 and the M14/41. Indeed. these types, despite heavy losses, remained the standard Italian medium tank throughout the war. The Italian L6/40 light tank also saw service in North Africa, Yugoslavia and Russia.

Overall, Mussolini's armour suffered several major shortcomings, being consistently too light, under-gunned and under-armoured. Initially the Italian forces in North Africa had very few tanks. In the Western Desert even the elderly British Rolls-Royce armoured car armed with the Boys anti-tank rifle could easily penetrate the L3's 12mm armour. Despite its obvious inadequacies, the L3 was to remain in service until 1943, well past its sell-by date.

The first Italian medium tank was developed just as war was breaking out. The M11/39 was armed with a turret-mounted 8mm Breda gun and a hull-mounted 37mm gun with a limited traverse of 30 degrees. In July 1940 seventy M11/39s were shipped to North Africa, where they formed the Italian 4th Tank Regiment. Unfortunately for the Italians, the M11/39 was mechanically unreliable, but during most of 1940 it was the only medium tank available to them. By December 1940 the 4th Tank Regiment only had twenty-three operational M11/39s available to oppose the inevitable British counter-attack; within months of the British campaign commencing, all the M11/39s were either destroyed or captured. By mid-1942 the Italians were mainly equipped with the M13/40 (only eighty-two M15/42s were built) but also began to receive new armour in the form of the 75/18 Semovente self-propelled gun.

While the Autoblinda AB40/41 series of armoured cars were better than their British counterparts, with good cross-country performance, they were not used to best effect. Instead of using them aggressively against the British, the Italians tended to deploy them for escort duties, with the Regia Aeronautica (Italian Air Force) being relied upon for reconnaissance work.

The standard Italian field gun of the day was the 75/27 75mm gun, which was inadequate by modern standards. The 105/28 gun was slightly better; acting as the standard battalion gun, it proved useful in North Africa. The 100/17 and 149/13 howitzers were common as well; both types were accurate, but their unwieldy trails made them unsuitable for modern warfare. The most effective weapon was the Ansaldo 75/46 anti-aircraft gun that could also act in an anti-tank role. Its low silhouette and clever camouflage meant that Allied tanks could close to within 500 yards before discovering it was there.

Mussolini's army, though, never really had a chance to prove itself. Poorly motivated, badly led and inadequately equipped, it was rapidly outclassed, which led to an inferiority complex among the troops. Nor was this something the Germans helped to dispel. With the loss of ten divisions and 130,000 men captured during 1940 and 1941, the Italian Army had received a body blow from which it could never recover, leaving Mussolini's armed forces subservient to Hitler.

Eventually Hitler decided to come to Mussolini's rescue in North Africa. On 12 February 1941 General Erwin Rommel arrived in Tripoli to command the Deutsches Afrika Korps (DAK) and the emphasis switched from Mussolini's weak armed forces to Hitler's powerful Wehrmacht. From this point on the fighting was to be of a very different nature. In Cyrenaica Mussolini assembled his remaining armoured forces, nominally independent of Rommel, consisting of the Corpo d'Armata di Manovra XX (20 Corps of Manoeuvre, or CAM), under General Gastone Gamara; this corps included the Ariete Armoured and Trieste Motorised Divisions.

Interestingly, it is worth noting that during the rest of the desert war much of the Axis armoured striking force belonged to Mussolini, with both the Ariete and Littorio Divisions playing an important part at Alamein. Mussolini eventually had three armoured divisions in North Africa (the 131st Centauro, 132nd Ariete and 133rd Littorio), as well as two motorised divisions (the 101st Trieste and 102nd Trente). All these forces were subordinate to German command and served Hitler's cause with mixed results.

The Ariete, the first Italian armoured division deployed to North Africa, did not arrive in Tripoli until January 1941 and was eventually destroyed at the second Battle of El Alamein. The Italians made their only attempt to create a true mechanised corps with the CAM in the summer of 1941. After serving in Yugoslavia, the Littorio Armoured Division arrived in North Africa in January 1942 but was also destroyed at El Alamein. The 131st Centauro served in Greece and Yugoslavia before being sent to Tripoli in November 1942; it finally surrendered in Tunisia in 1943.

Once Rommel took charge, Mussolini's troops showed a marked improvement in confidence and performance. During the Axis reconquest of Cyrenaica on 7 April 1941 units of the Ariete captured 2,000 men from an Indian brigade, while at Halfaya Pass the Italian gunners gave a good account of themselves by knocking out seven British tanks. Utilising German tactics, Italian potential briefly flared at Bir el Gobi on 19 November 1941, when no fewer than 137 M13/40 medium tanks from the Ariete, with artillery support, threw back 159 British Crusader Mk VIs, claiming fifty kills. This British rebuff was partly due to their contempt of Italian capabilities, based on previous experience at Beda Fomm.

At the second Battle of El Alamein Mussolini's armour was simply outclassed. His armoured and motorised corps fought with great bravery but to no avail. As Rommel observed, 'The Italian anti-tank guns were simply useless against the heavy British armour.' British tanks were able to stand off at ranges between 2,000 and 2,700 yards and simply pick off the Axis guns and tanks, which could not penetrate the British armour at that range. Copious supplies of ammunition also meant that the British tanks could pour up to thirty rounds into a single target.

The Italian 47mm anti-tank gun was no more effective than the German 50mm, and as a result the tanks of the Littorio and Trieste Divisions were swiftly knocked out and the units put to flight. The Ariete Armoured Division was surrounded, with predictable results. Rommel lamented the destruction of his oldest Italian comrades. The Italian 20th Motorised Division escaped with just ten tanks, which were deployed along with the eleven German tanks in Rommel's mobile reserve for the defence of Sollum. General Messe, who had commanded the Italian Expeditionary Corps in Russia, was sent to take charge of the Italian troops in North Africa.

By 1940, with almost half a million men under arms in Abyssinia (Ethiopia), Eritrea, Italian Somaliland and Libya, the Italian dictator Benito Mussolini considered himself the strong man of Africa. (*Author's Collection*)

Hitler's Blitzkrieg through northern France in May 1940 proved unstoppable, as this wrecked Char B1 tank testifies; the swift defeat of the French Army that summer gave Mussolini a free hand to attack British interests in North Africa. (*Author's Collection*)

A Renault R-35 light tank firing in the French Alps; somewhat belatedly Mussolini joined Hitler's attack on France on 11 June 1940, but his forces made little impression against just six French divisions. Only when Hitler's panzers came sweeping down the Rhone Valley could Mussolini claim victory. The Franco–German armistice was signed on 22 June 1940, followed by the Franco–Italian Armistice two days later, and the war in France officially came to an end. (*Author's Collection*)

French West African troops captured in France. Following the Axis armistice with France, Mussolini was content that French colonial forces in Tunisia posed no threat to his position in Libya, allowing him to turn his back on them and attack British forces in Egypt. (*Normandie Collection*)

(*Above*) This was the reality of Mussolini's armoured forces. The two-man Fiat-Ansaldo turretless Carro Veloce ('Fast Tank' or tankette) CV.33 appeared in 1933; it was armed with machine-guns, weighed in at 3.5 tons and had a top speed of 28mph and was really only sufficient for police duties. Two years later it was followed by the slightly improved CV.35 and with the introduction of standard designations (type, weight, year) they became the L3/33 and L3/35 respectively, assigned to infantry support and reconnaissance roles. While the former was armed with a 6.5mm machine-gun and protected by just 12mm of armour, the latter had bolted rather than riveted armour and was equipped with twin 8mm machine-guns. In 1940 the tiny L3 formed the bulk of Mussolini's tank forces. It equipped three Italian armoured divisions, the tank battalions of the motorised divisions and the tank squadrons of the *Celere* or fast divisions. In stark contrast, there were just two battalions with the M11/39. The L3's combat track record in Ethiopia and Spain was not very good. (*Author's Collection*)

(*Opposite, top*) On the eve of war this was the face of Mussolini's medium tank force but it was hardly comparable to Hitler's Panzer Mk III and IV. The Fiat-Ansaldo M11/39 medium tank was little more than an up-gunned light tank. While its 37mm gun was quite respectable for the late 1930s, the size of the turret meant that the main gun was placed in the hull, greatly limiting its traverse. Like many tanks of the day it suffered from poor mechanical reliability and its 30mm armour could not withstand the British 2-pounder anti-tank gun. Against the British Mk VI light tank, which was armed with just a machine-gun, the M11/39 was quite effective. However, against the British A series Cruiser and Matilda tanks it was completely outclassed and the crews quite often abandoned the M11/39 in the face of attack. To make matters worse for the Italians, only a hundred were ever produced. (*Author's Collection*)

(*Right*) The M13/40, designed to replace the Italian L3, L6/40 and M11/39, was a much better tank but suffered the same reliability problems as well as insufficient armament and armour. While the 47mm gun could handle British light and Cruiser tanks, it could not deal with anything heavier. The sandbags heaped on the front of the hull were a crude way of supplementing the 40mm armour. (*Australian Army*)

The Fiat L6/40 light tank was a development of the L3 tankette, having gone through a number of prototypes in the late 1930s. Originally intended as an export product armed with a 37mm gun, when it finally went into production it had a turret-mounted 20mm gun and an 8mm coaxial machine-gun. Already obsolete when it entered service in 1941, its low silhouette nevertheless made it useful in the reconnaissance role and it saw action toward the end of the North African campaign. (*Author's Collection*)

Less than cheerful-looking Italian mechanics photographed in Libya; the Italian Army was far from mechanised and was not really capable of taking on even Britain's weak military units but this did not stop Mussolini attacking British interests in both North and East Africa. (*L.J. Alexander/Corporal Eric Evans RASC*)

An Italian gunner on guard duty at an artillery depot in Libya; the Italian Army had a good number of 75mm and 100mm guns in North Africa but mobility was a problem, as was tactical deployment. The standard Italian field gun was the inadequate 75/27 75mm gun. This could only manage a range of 9,000 yards, and in order to achieve this a pit had to be dug for the trail to gain the required elevation. Also its shells had poor fragmentation qualities. (*L.J. Alexander/Corporal Eric Evans RASC*)

Italian gunners strike a pose with their ancient fortress muzzle-loading guns. Many of these weapons ended up being deployed as decoys to draw British fire away from more worthwhile targets. (*L.J. Alexander/Corporal Eric Evans RASC*)

Italian gunners exercising with 75mm or 100mm field guns. The British were to capture 400 guns at Bardia alone that were simply abandoned by the fleeing gunners. (*Paul Lazell/Sergeant Bill Lazell RA*)

The Autoblinda 41 or AB 41 4x4 armoured car (essentially an up-gunned AB40) had a turret similar to the L6/40 carrying a 20mm Breda 35 autocannon; it also had a coaxial 8mm machine-gun and another one in the rear. This armoured car served with the Italian Army in North Africa but plans to upgrade it with a 47mm anti-tank gun did not come to fruition. Sand tyres greatly extended its mobility. (*Author's Collection*)

An improved version of the M13/40, known as the M14/41, appeared in 1941, though it was essentially the same tank. While it used the same chassis, it had a redesigned hull, thicker armour and a more powerful engine. A further upgrade produced the M15/42 but this did not go into production until 1943 and all examples were confiscated by Hitler after he occupied Italy. (*Author's Collection*)

In 1942, in an attempt to bolster their inadequate M13 and M14 tanks, the Italians introduced the Semovente 75/18 assault gun in an effort to emulate the success of the German Sturmgeschütz. These were issued to one company in each of the tank battalions. Armed with a 75mm mountain gun, they proved quite effective against the American Grant and Sherman tanks. (*Author's Collection*)

Chapter Two

The Western Desert Force

Churchill was not blind to the very real danger that Mussolini might drive the under-strength British forces out of western Egypt and back across the strategically vital Suez Canal. In reality, Mussolini's Italian panzers were to prove a pale shadow of their German cousins wreaking havoc throughout Europe, but at the time Churchill had no way of knowing this. Ironically, it was the inadequacy of Mussolini's armour that was to embroil Hitler in this secondary theatre of operations. What Churchill did know was that Hitler was threatening Britain from across the English Channel, while Mussolini was greedily eyeing British interests in Africa.

Following the 1938 'Munich Crisis' a British mobile force had been put together in Egypt, but its capabilities were so limited that it had been dubbed the 'immobile farce'. By the following year it was supposed to be an armoured division, but equipped as it was with various marks of Vickers light tanks, some 1920-pattern Rolls-Royce armoured cars and a few old Vickers medium tanks, it clearly lacked punch. One armoured regiment had to make do with machine-guns, lorries and 3.7-inch mountain guns towed by tracked 'Dragons'.

By the time war broke out the Western Desert Force (the predecessor of the Eighth Army), under Major General Richard O'Connor (who answered to General Archibald Wavell as Commander-in-Chief Middle East), had expanded to include the 7th Armoured Division, soon to become known as the 'Desert Rats', equipped with A9 and A10 Cruiser tanks as well as Mk VI light tanks. Most notably the 7th Royal Tank Regiment (RTR) was equipped with the much heavier Matilda infantry-support tank. Prior to the Italian offensive, the Cruiser tanks were withdrawn from the frontier. Amidst sporadic skirmishing, a lone squadron of tanks was left behind to watch the border, along with some armoured cars.

At the outbreak of hostilities Churchill had fewer than 10,000 men available to protect Egypt, so a series of aggressive operations were conducted to keep the Italians firmly off balance. Maddalena and Capuzzo were temporarily seized on 14 June 1940. Three days later the Western Desert Force was created out of the HQ of 6th Division under Major General Richard O'Connor. He had only the 4th

Armoured Brigade, comprising two tank and two artillery regiments, and two infantry battalions in the immediate vicinity of Mersa Matruh.

When Italy declared war, the RAF's Desert Air Force (DAF) could muster a few Gladiator fighters, some Blenheim medium bombers and a few Wellington and Bombay medium bombers based in Egypt. From the start they aggressively attacked enemy airfields, the Italian air base at El Adem outside Tobruk being raided on the first day of the war.

By the summer of 1940, despite the low priority placed on tank production in British factories, Britain's armoured units possessed about 240 medium and 108 Cruiser tanks, as well as 514 light tanks. As the fighting with the Italians in North Africa escalated, many were dispatched to Egypt. In October 1940 Churchill's reinforcements began to arrive in Egypt, the most significant of which were fifty Matilda infantry-support tanks. This was the most powerful weapon in the British tank inventory and its 80mm frontal armour could withstand every Italian gun in service.

Churchill's ill-fated attempts to help Greece as well as distract Mussolini and Hitler from North Africa meant that he effectively threw away the victory at Beda Fomm. The 1st Armoured Brigade, the New Zealand Division and the 6th Australian Division, fully equipped at the expense of those forces in North Africa, were dispatched to Greece in early March 1941. The 1st Armoured Brigade consisted of the light tanks of the 4th Hussars and the Matildas of the 3rd Royal Tank Regiment, plus infantry, anti-tank guns and artillery. Mussolini's armour may have been no threat to Churchill's tanks, but the Greek terrain and Hitler's panzers proved fatal.

Following its victory over the Italians in North Africa in early 1941, the British 7th Armoured Division was withdrawn to Egypt for a refit just as General Erwin Rommel's Afrika Korps was arriving in Libya. The replacement 2nd Armoured Division comprised the Divisional Support Group and the 3rd Armoured Brigade, the latter with just eighty-six of its 156 tanks. There could be no hiding the fact that the 2nd Armoured Division was an improvised formation equipped with a regiment of inadequate Cruiser tanks, a regiment of equally useless light tanks and a regiment using captured Italian tanks. In particular, the 6th Royal Tank Regiment (6RTR) was issued with Italian M13s, which had been repaired but lacked radios. All of this equipment was swiftly to end up in Rommel's hands.

In mid-May 1941 Wavell's tank force was increased by 135 Matildas, eighty-two Cruisers (fifty of which were brand-new Cruiser Mk VI (A15) Crusader Is — enough to re-equip a whole tank regiment), and twenty-one light tanks. All these tanks except the Crusaders were slow. While the Germans and Italians respected the Matilda, the Crusader I, which came with Churchill's 'Tiger' convoy, carried the same inadequate 2-pounder gun and its superior cross-country handling was nullified by niggling engine problems. The Crusader had been rushed into service before its teething problems could be ironed out, and it suffered from the same defects as its predecessors, principally thin armour and mechanical unreliability. While it was fast (with the right modifications it could manage up to 40mph in the desert), the engine was elderly and suffered from clogged air filters and other cooling problems, especially with the fan's drive shafts.

Churchill was keen to strike back at Rommel immediately, but to his irritation he found that once in Egypt his 'Cubs' had to be worked up in the workshops, with sand filters fitted and the cooling systems modified. The mechanics had to wade through voluminous manuals to pick up all the important manufacturers' do's and don'ts. Despite the Crusaders' and Mark IV's (A13) shortcomings, these tanks were issued to Major General Michael O'Moore Creagh's 7th Armoured Division. This unit had been without tanks for four months, so needed time to familiarise itself, particularly with the Crusader.

By September 1941 13 Corps had been reinforced by 30 Corps to form the Eighth Army under General Cunningham. The 7th Armoured Division was now mainly composed of Crusaders, but still had some A13s and some even older Cruiser tanks, while the 4th Armoured Brigade consisted entirely of American-supplied Stuart light tanks known by the British as 'Honeys'. The two army tank brigades (one with 13 Corps and the other with the Tobruk garrison) had a combination of Matilda and Valentine tanks. The South African Marmon-Herrington Mk II was the main armoured car, while American and Canadian vehicles were gradually introduced to phase out older British models. By November 1941 the second generation of British infantry and Cruiser tanks, along with American light tanks, had reached North Africa.

The 1st Armoured Division learned the hard way not to under-estimate Rommel's capabilities. In January 1942 his forces first enveloped and then put to flight its divisional combat group, which lost three-quarters of its 150 tanks along with eighty-five guns. While most armoured units moved as whole divisions or tank brigades, part of the ill-fated 2nd Armoured Division ended up in Greece and a brigade from the 1st Armoured Division was incorporated into the 7th Armoured Division for the Crusader operation. Likewise, heavy losses sometimes meant the end of units, such as the 7th Armoured Brigade in early 1942 and the 8th Armoured Division just before Alamein (where its HQ was used to fool Rommel). By the time of Alamein the Eighth Army included the 1st, 7th and 10th Armoured Divisions.

Commonwealth support for the war in the Western Desert was considerable, with the 6th and 9th Australian Divisions, the New Zealand Division, the 1st and 2nd South African Divisions and various aviation and naval units all seeing action. Likewise the Indian Army supplied the 4th and 5th Indian Divisions under British officers. They all included armoured support units.

(*Above*) 'In June 1940, when the British Empire seemed to Fascist eyes reeling to ruin, and France was almost prostrate, the Italian Empire in Africa spread far and wide,' warned British Prime Minister Winston Churchill. 'Libya, Eritrea, Abyssinia [Ethiopia], Somaliland, ... comprised a vast region ... under the protection of more than 400,000 Italian and native troops.' (*Author's Collection*)

(*Opposite, top*) Britain's paucity of tanks at the outbreak of war was a glaring deficiency for the British Army. Those tanks available were too lightly armoured and their guns lacked the punch necessary to tackle Hitler's panzers on anything like equal terms. Most of the British Expeditionary Force's tank strength deployed in France in 1940 comprised the Mk VIB light tank. Although designed for reconnaissance, it was often used in a Cruiser role, its inadequate armour and armament invariably leading to heavy losses when facing anything heavier than a Panzer Mk I. (*Author's Collection*)

(*Opposite, below*) The Matilda Mk II infantry tank was the best tank in the British inventory. Designed in the mid-1930s by Colonel Hudson's team at the Mechanisation Board, it benefited from work conducted on the A7 medium tank (which never saw the light of day). In late 1937 some 165 Matilda IIs were ordered, but due to the shape and size of the armour castings the tank was not easy to mass-produce. When war broke out in 1939 there were just two in service. Although heavily armoured (with some 78mm of armour on the front, more than twice as much as the Panzer II and III), across country it was slow and its 2-pounder (40mm) main armament lacked real penetrating power. However, in North Africa it was to prove the British Army's saviour against the Italians. (*Author's Collection*)

The Mk VIB, armed with just two Vickers machine-guns, was the most numerous British tank by the late 1930s and it provided the majority of the tanks in service with the British Army in France and the Western Desert. (*Author's Collection*)

This side view of the Mk VIB light tank is believed to have been taken in the Western Desert. This was the final development of the Carden-Loyd series, mounting one .50-inch and one .303-inch Vickers machine-gun in the turret which this crewman is sitting on. (*L.J. Alexander/Corporal Eric Evans RASC*)

The early British Cruiser tanks, the A9, A10 and A13, were too slow and too thinly armoured. This A13 Mk II was the last of the series to see combat and the type was issued to the 7th Armoured Division (the Mk III Covenanter was relegated to training duties in the UK). Britain's Cruiser tanks were withdrawn from the Egyptian–Libyan frontier in anticipation of an attack by Mussolini. (*Author's Collection*)

At the outbreak of war the British Army had seventy-six First World War vintage Rolls-Royce armoured cars still in service, some of which were in Egypt. These included the 1920 (seen here) and 1924 Pattern variants, though these were withdrawn from the front line at the end of 1941. Some thirty-four vehicles in service with the 11th Hussars had an open-topped turret fitted to allow them to carry the Boys anti-tank rifle and the Bren light machine-gun. Amidst sporadic skirmishing, a lone squadron of British tanks was left behind to watch the border, along with some armoured cars. (*Paul Lazell/Sergeant Bill Lazell RA*)

The British Army went to war with wholly inadequate anti-tank guns, principally the 2-pounder (40mm) developed in the mid-1930s and the 6-pounder (57mm) developed in the late 1930s. Crucially the latter did not enter production until 1941 because the War Office insisted on replacing those 2-pounders lost in France. This gun belonged to Private Adam Wakenshaw, who gained a posthumous VC for knocking out a German self-propelled gun. (*Steve Hunnisett/Ron Hunnisett RA*)

The very advanced 25-pounder had replaced the First World War vintage 18-pounder field gun and the 4.5-inch howitzer as the standard field artillery weapon by the time of the North African campaign. It could be emplaced in one minute, and had a lightweight firing platform which allowed a rapid all-round traverse (a valuable asset when fighting tanks). This particular gun was knocked out during the battle of El Alamein. (*Steve Hunnisett/Ron Hunnisett RA*)

Along with Gibraltar and Malta in the Mediterranean, the Egyptian port at Alexandria (seen here) provided key naval facilities for the Royal Navy and was vital in keeping the British Army in North Africa resupplied. Similarly, once Hitler committed his forces to support Mussolini in North Africa, Rommel became reliant on the port of Tripoli. (*Author's Collection*)

Getting troops and supply ships to Alexandria became a major preoccupation for Churchill and his commanders. (*Author's Collection*)

The island of Malta, sitting in the middle of the Mediterranean, made it a key Royal Navy communications hub for the British convoys en route to Alexandria, which normally stopped off here. Sustaining the island became a major task in itself. Here supplies are hurriedly unloaded at night by arc-light from a freighter docked in Malta's Grand Harbour. (*Author's Collection*)

Malta's proximity to Sicily ensured that it became one of the most heavily bombed places on the face of the Earth thanks to the Luftwaffe and the Regia Aeronautica (Italian Air Force). Valletta and the docks at Grand Harbour suffered intensive bombing. Here the island's anti-aircraft batteries ward off yet another attack. (*Author's Collection*)

At the far end of the Mediterranean Britain also had bases on Cyprus and in Palestine. These locally raised infantry were drawn from Arab and Jewish volunteers. This helped facilitate British attacks on pro-Nazi Iraq and Vichy-controlled Lebanon and Syria. (*Author's Collection*)

The British Army had a liking for tracked carriers. The first, bearing the Vickers machine-gun, appeared in 1935, and the subsequent Carrier Bren was then superseded by the Carrier Universal from 1940, though the generic name 'Bren Carrier' stuck. It was directed by a steering wheel, which made driver training much easier. Maximum hull armour went up to 12mm, though the crew and passenger compartments remained open. Other variants included the Cavalry Carrier and the Scout Carrier (only fifty of the former were built, whereas the latter numbered 667). The British Carrier was used widely by units in North Africa. (*Author's Collection*)

A South African-built Mk II Marmon-Herrington armoured car serving with the French Flying Column No. 1. Two variants of the Mk II were built, the MFF type, which numbered 549 for the Union Defence Force's Mobile Field Force (hence MFF), and the ME type, which totalled 338 built for the Middle East campaign. South Africa also built 2,630 Mk III and 936 Mk IV armoured cars during the period 1941–44. In total the South Africans manufactured about 5,750 armoured cars during the course of the war, which provided a welcome stop-gap for the desperate troops in North Africa. (*Author's Collection*)

Access to water during the fighting in North Africa was vital and meant that all the desert watering holes took on special significance. This is the oasis at Al Jahgbub. (*L.J. Alexander/Corporal Eric Evans RASC*)

The open tank country was also ideal for the sowing of land mines, and sappers were to play a vital role in countering Axis defensive measures. (*Author's Collection*)

These Australian soldiers are trudging through the midday heat of the Western Desert. While the vast, seemingly endless, expanses of barren desert were ideal tank country, features such as the Qattara Depression and Ruweisat Ridge provided useful natural defensive barriers. (*Author's Collection*)

Both sides were to consider the air war in North Africa of secondary importance as there were greater strategic concerns elsewhere. Fortunately for the RAF, the Italians had inferior planes. While the Luftwaffe had better-quality aircraft, most notably the Messerschmitt Bf-109 that was superior to both the Hurricane (seen here) and the American-supplied Tomahawk, their numbers were never sufficient to tilt the balance. (*Author's Collection*)

Following Britain's humiliating expulsion from France in June 1940, and the loss of most of the British Army's tanks, Churchill looked to America for help. He wanted the Americans to build British tanks but instead he found the M3 medium tank, which was similar in concept to the Italian M11 but carried a far more powerful gun. (*US Army/NARA*)

The M3 Grant, while far from perfect, was to prove an ideal stopgap remedy to the firepower of Rommel's panzers and was just what the Eighth Army needed. Once America's industries had ramped up production, Montgomery did the rest. (*US Army/NARA*)

Chapter Three

'Fox killed in the open' – Beda Fomm

After Mussolini's declaration of war on 10 June 1940 it seemed certain that he would strike eastward from the port of Bardia and Fort Capuzzo in Libya with the intention of seizing the strategically vital railhead 50 miles away at Mersa Matruh in Egypt. His Fifth Army, equivalent to nine divisions, was stationed in Tripolitania (western Libya) and initially guarded the French Tunisian border, but after the fall of France and the formation of the pro-German Vichy government Tunisia no longer posed any threat, although Mussolini soon came to fear the Free French in Equatorial Africa. His Tenth Army in Cyrenaica (eastern Libya), consisting of five divisions, was bolstered with four divisions from the Fifth Army in June 1940, bringing Mussolini's forces facing Egypt up to about 250,000 men.

General d'Armata Berti's Tenth Army was scheduled to move against Sollum, Halfaya Pass and Sidi Barrani in August with 21 Corps, consisting of three divisions supported by the Libyan divisions and the Motorised Maletti Group. The attack, though, never took place and in Tripoli Marshal Maresciallo Graziani, the Italian Commander-in-Chief North Africa, came under increasing pressure from an exasperated Mussolini who had hoped to emulate Hitler's Blitzkrieg across France.

Graziani was finally forced to launch his attack the following month. Ironically, those divisions with desert experience were in Albania preparing for Mussolini's foolhardy invasion of Greece. Graziani massed six divisions, with Libyan troops spearheading General Annabale Bergonzoli's 23 Corps supported by the Maletti Group, which was to act as flank guard. The offensive commenced on 13 September 1940 with Graziani commanding the operation from way back at Tobruk, using inadequate radio communication.

Bergonzoli's 'Blitzkrieg' advanced 65 miles into Egypt before his men dug in at Sidi Barrani and refused to go any further for lack of armour and artillery. Back in London Churchill and his generals were able to heave a sigh of relief; clearly Mussolini was living up to his reputation for bluff and bluster. The British Western Desert Force was given a valuable breathing space – and a clear indication of the poor standard of Italian leadership.

Some 36,000 men under General Wavell launched a counter-raid that soon developed into a full offensive. The Italians, outmatched and poorly motivated, initially did not know how to conduct armoured warfare against the British. Slowly their performance improved but they had to learn the hard way and then it was largely too late.

At Alam Nibeiwa on 9 December 1940 General Pietro Maletti's artillery continued to fire ineffectively until overrun by British tanks, while at Sidi Barrani and Bardia the British armour caused widespread panic. All the M11/39s were taken by surprise and were destroyed without a fight by the advancing Matildas at Nibeiwa. General Richard O'Connor slipped behind the Italians and their defences simply collapsed.

The 4th Indian Division recorded that at Nibeiwa,

Frightened, dazed or desperate Italians erupted from tents and slit trenches, some to surrender supinely, others to leap gallantly into battle, hurling grenades or blazing machine-guns in futile belabour of the impregnable intruders ... General Maletti, the Italian commander, sprang from his dug-out, machine-gun in hand. He fell from an answering burst; his son beside him was struck down and captured.

The Italians valiantly resisted for another two-and-a-half hours and one British tank crewman was struck by their courage: 'The Italians may have been a push-over afterwards, but they fought like hell at Nibeiwa.'

O'Connor and Wavell launched their counter-stroke, Operation Compass, on 9 December 1940, employing the virtually impregnable Matilda infantry tank to roll the Italians completely out of Egypt. In just three days they captured 38,000 Italian and Libyan troops, 73 tanks, 1,000 vehicles and 237 guns. Bardia fell to the British on 3 January 1941, yielding another 40,000 Italian troops; likewise Tobruk fell on the 22nd and gave up 27,000 prisoners, 90 tanks, 200 vehicles and 200 guns of various calibres.

Following his defeat General Graziani, full of doom and gloom, wrote to his wife, 'One cannot break steel armour with finger nails alone.' He considered withdrawing on Tripoli but Mussolini would have none of it, raging, 'This man has lost his mind or at least his senses. Here is another man with whom I cannot get angry, because I despise him.' Mussolini's remaining forces were dramatically cut off at Beda Fomm in early February 1941. General Guiseppe Tellera, Commander-in-Chief of the Tenth Army, lost 21,000 men. O'Connor sent Wavell a message that summed up the end of Mussolini's aspirations in North Africa; it simply read 'Fox killed in the open.'

Trooper 'Topper' Brown of the 2nd Royal Tank Regiment was in the thick of it: 'Practically all morning we never stopped firing, at wagon-loads of infantry or tanks. I haven't a clue how many enemy I killed, but it must have run into hundreds. We definitely had a score of twenty M13s at the end of the day ...' He took out the last M13 with his final two rounds: 'We had started out with 112 rounds of 2-pounder,

97 in the racks and 15 extra. Hughes had let us get down to the last two . . . so you can understand the amount of firing I had done.'

General Valentino Babini's armoured brigade had only a few days to become familiar with the newly arrived replacement M13/40 tanks. Again these were too lightly armoured and lacked radios. Over a hundred were found around Beda Fomm, some burnt out but many simply abandoned by inexperienced crews. 'You were too soon, that is all,' said General Bergonzoli, when questioned by his British captors about his army's performance. 'But we gave battle at once . . . And always, here as everywhere else, we were grossly outnumbered. So when our second attack was unable to prevail we had no choice but to make an honourable surrender.'

The King's Royal Rifles passed through the scene of destruction:

> After we had gone a few miles south . . . we came upon the scene . . . an imposing mess of shattered Italian tanks, abandoned guns and derelict lorries. There was the familiar sight of hordes of prisoners being rounded up; processions of staff cars, containing General Bergonzoli and his entourage, passed up the road towards Benghazi.

Wavell understandably was full of praise for his troops' efforts: 'The Army of the Nile, as our Prime Minister has called us, has in two months advanced over 400 miles, has destroyed the large army that had gathered to invade Egypt, taking some 125,000 prisoners and well over 1,000 guns besides innumerable quantities of weapons and material of all kinds. These achievements will always be remembered.'

In Britain the newspapers triumphantly ran with the headline 'Wavell's Wave Sweeps over Libya.'

By now Mussolini's forces were in complete disarray. Hitler's Blitzkrieg by proxy in North Africa had ended as a complete and utter shambles, leaving Churchill occupying half of Libya. In total Mussolini's Tenth Army had lost 130,000 prisoners, almost 500 tanks and thousands of wheeled vehicles. The Italian Army was left reeling and Mussolini was furious that his military might had been squandered.

O'Connor was understandably disappointed that he was not allowed to have a go at capturing Tripoli. When asked if he could have taken it, he responded,

> I think we could have done so at once, or fairly shortly after, before the Luftwaffe came into the picture. Of course, the question of supplies would have been difficult. But this would have been greatly eased by the Italian rations, which we could have picked up at Sirte and Tripoli. Like the rest of the campaign it would have been a risk, but I think personally not a dangerous one.

O'Connor's dramatic victory at Beda Fomm was the defining moment of the first round of the war in North Africa. 'Thus ended', said Churchill, 'Mussolini's dream of an African Empire to be built by conquest and colonised in the spirit of ancient Rome.'

Mussolini in benevolent mood. It seemed certain that the Italian Tenth Army would invade Egypt in the summer of 1941 with the intention of seizing the railhead at Mersa Matruh. However, Mussolini was soon frustrated by the cautiousness of his generals. (*Author's Collection*)

The painting on this barrack block in Libya shows how Italy under Mussolini saw its position in the Mediterranean – as one of dominance. (*L.J. Alexander/Corporal Eric Evans RASC*)

'A British dugout near Mersa' says the caption to this photograph, but it isn't clear whether it means the forward advance base of Mersa Matruh or Mersa el Brega in Libya. Unfortunately for the British there was a 25-mile gap in the road between Alexandria and Mersa Matruh, and the railway was only a single line. (*L.J. Alexander/Corporal Eric Evans RASC*)

The Italian Army's Blitzkrieg got as far as Sidi Barrani in Egypt. They made a fatal mistake in their dispositions south of the town in the Enba Gap, a 20-mile unprotected stretch of desert lying between the fortified Italian camps of Nibeiwa and Rabia. It was here that Wavell and O'Connor would strike. (*L.J. Alexander/Corporal Eric Evans RASC*)

The M11s were too few in number to have any great impact on the battle and their thin, riveted armour easily fell prey to British tanks when it went up against them. Not surprisingly, the few that survived the fighting were quickly withdrawn from service. (*Author's Collection*)

Too little, too late – a brand-new M13/40 tank being unloaded in Libya. Luckily for the British tanks, the Babini Armoured Brigade (which was potentially stronger than the 7th Armoured Division) acted defensively rather than offensively. These tanks were rushed into combat, giving the crews little time to familiarise themselves with them, and the M13s' lack of radios greatly hampered unit coordination. (*Author's Collection*)

Heavy Italian artillery, such as these ancient 150mm guns, was soon abandoned in the face of British counter-attack. (*L.J. Alexander/Corporal Eric Evans RASC*)

British carriers and Mk VIB light tanks moving up: the rapidity of the Western Desert Force's advance astonished everyone. In places, such as Nibeiwa, the Italians fought bravely until they were overrun by British tanks, but afterwards they just seemed to give up. (*Author's Collection*)

British Cruiser tanks such as these A9s were adequate for fighting the Italian Army but were clearly outclassed by the time the Afrika Korps arrived in Libya. The A9's main armament was a 2-pounder gun, though a few were armed with 3.7-inch howitzers for the close-support role. The A9 had the distinction of being the first British tank to have a power-operated turret and an auxiliary engine. However, it proved too slow and too lightly armoured to be a successful design. (*Author's Collection*)

Sollum, Bardia, Tobruk and Derna: milestones along the route of the victorious Eighth Army. Here British infantry are 'debussing' in Bardia. This Libyan port changed hands numerous times during the North African campaign, but was first captured by the British from the Italians on 3 January 1941. (*Author's Collection*)

A desert dug-out near Bardia; according to the notice, it is under the new management of Young & Jackson's. Mussolini lost 40,000 men at Bardia and another 27,000 at Tobruk. (*L.J. Alexander/Corporal Eric Evans RASC*)

The lumbering Matilda II provided a nasty shock for the Italians as its frontal armour could withstand every Italian gun in service, leaving flight or surrender as the only options. When Rommel arrived in North Africa the following year he made sure that his troops were equipped to deal with the troublesome Matilda II. (*Author's Collection*)

A British Army column stops for a breather. The speed with which the Italian Army collapsed took both O'Connor and Wavell by surprise. O'Connor was all for pressing on to Tripoli but Churchill insisted on helping the Greeks, which diverted resources. (*L.J. Alexander/Corporal Eric Evans RASC*)

An Italian L3 lies abandoned by the Mediterranean Sea without a mark on it. Some L3s were modified to carry a 20mm anti-tank rifle instead of the standard machine-guns and these also saw service in North Africa. Designated the L3cc ('controcarro' or anti-tank), examples were captured outside Bardia in 1941. Similarly a number of L3s were converted to the flamethrower role. (*Author's Collection*)

Italian 75mm artillery strewn across the desert after the capture of Bardia by British forces. The Italians lost not only large numbers of men but also vast quantities of equipment. (*Author's Collection*)

This Italian gunner probably lost his life or was captured during the rout of the Italian Army in Egypt and Cyrenaica. (*L.J. Alexander/Corporal Eric Evans RASC*)

British officers examine abandoned M13/40 tanks in the Benghazi area. Judging by the tanks' condition and position, they had broken down rather than been knocked out. Over a hundred of these tanks were found around Beda Fomm, some burnt out, but most simply abandoned. (*Author's Collection*)

During the early operations over Libya the Fiat CR.42 Falco (Falcon) fighter enjoyed a slight edge over the RAF's fighters, but as British forces built up the aircraft was restricted largely to ground-support activities along with the older CR.32. The CR.42 was the most numerous fighter possessed by the Regia Aeronautica in North Africa. The Italian G.50 was not a great success. The Macchi Saetta and Folgore were an improvement, but were still no match for Allied fighters. Throughout the 1940–41 campaign more Italian aircraft were destroyed on the ground than in aerial combat. (*L.J. Alexander/Corporal Eric Evans RASC*)

A British soldier stands guard over the smouldering remains of what looks to be either an Italian Fiat G.50 or a Saetta fighter aircraft. (*Author's Collection*)

Corporal Ronald Hunnisett poses in front of a captured Italian Spa TL37 4x4 light truck. This variant is the AS37 or Autocarro Sahariano; other versions included the long-range desert reconnaissance vehicle known as the AS43 Camionetta Desertica. (*Steve Hunnisett/Corporal Ron Hunnisett RA*)

Another abandoned M13/40. The tanks captured at Beda Fomm were found to have come from the Ariete and Centauro Armoured Regiments. These units had been forced to send many of their tanks to replace the catastrophic losses of earlier in the campaign. The 2nd Royal Tank Regiment made short work of them. (*Author's Collection*)

ROAD DISTANCE MILES
SIDI BARRANI 95
BUQ BUQ 120
SALUM 145
BARDIA 165
TOBRUK 243
GAZALA 285
DERNA 358
BARCE 490
BENGHASI 550

British troops gathered under a road sign marking all the major battle sites in North Africa. (*Author's Collection*)

February 1941 brought a dispiriting end to Mussolini's dream of driving on Cairo and Suez. The Italian Army never really recovered from its humiliating defeat of late 1940/early 1941. (*Author's Collection*)

Chapter Four

East African Distraction

In Abyssinia (modern-day Ethiopia), Eritrea and Italian Somaliland Mussolini had 200,000 men under the Duke of Aosta. Fortunately for the British, the Italian Army in East Africa had few tanks. In total they mustered about twenty-four inadequate M11/39 medium tanks and thirty-five L3 light tanks, none of which constituted much of a threat. Only a hundred M11/39s were ever built and the bulk of these had gone to Libya. One of the few armoured car types available to the Italian forces in East Africa was the Autoblindo Mitragliatrice Lanzia Ansaldo IZ.

The Lancia IZ armoured car first went into service in 1915 but saw very little action until two years later. It was fitted with a number of different turret types, including a double version with one on top of the other, with two machine-guns in the larger lower turret and one in the smaller upper one. Weighing in at around 4 tons, it could manage less than 40mph, so was hardly fast; additionally its armour was very thin. Nevertheless, the vehicle proved robust and went on to see action during the Spanish Civil War, while some were also deployed to North Africa for policing duties. However, despite their longevity, only 120 IZ armoured cars were ever produced so there cannot have been many of them in East Africa. Local police units there may also have been equipped with a few equally ancient Bianchi armoured cars, which were likewise veterans of the First World War. Certainly numbers of these were captured in Cyrenaica by the British.

Mussolini's colonial troops in Italian East Africa were formed into provisional divisions, though they fought largely as independent brigades; in Eritrea these troops consisted of the 1st–4th Colonial Divisions, with the 101st and 102nd Colonial Divisions in Somaliland. They could strike north into Sudan, which was garrisoned by just 9,000 British and colonial troops; south into Kenya, which was defended by 8,500 men, or north-east into British Somaliland, which was protected by a mere 537 soldiers. However, Mussolini's efforts against the British in East Africa during 1940 were half-hearted at best. In July some 6,500 Italian troops supported by two dozen tanks occupied Kassala, just 12 miles inside Sudan. Since the British garrison for the whole of Sudan consisted of just three infantry battalions, they prudently avoided battle.

The following month Mussolini attacked British Somaliland, which was trapped between Italian Somaliland to the west and Abyssinia to the south, with a force of twenty-six battalions also supported by tanks and artillery. The vastly outnumbered but determined British defenders at the Tug Argan Pass, leading to the port of Berbera, held the Italians at bay for four days. Mussolini's troops suffered 2,000 casualties for the loss of just 250 British troops. The British then conducted a sea-borne evacuation from Berbera to Kenya, where a British build-up was taking place ready for a knock-out counter-offensive. At the same time British forces in Egypt were also preparing to counter-attack the Italians, who had dug in just inside the frontier.

Lieutenant General Sir Alan Cunningham took charge in Kenya in November 1940 and soon had 75,000 men under arms; it was a truly cosmopolitan force, comprising 27,000 South Africans, 33,000 East Africans, 9,000 West Africans and about 6,000 British. They were equipped with some tracked carriers and a few armoured cars, but little else. The Italian troops in East Africa came up against British armoured cars of unknown origin in early 1941. They were in fact of South African and Kenyan manufacture.

Following Dunkirk, the British were desperately short of armoured fighting vehicles and turned to South Africa for help. In response, the South Africans produced the Mark I and II Marmon-Herrington armoured cars based on the Ford 3-ton chassis. Those sent to East Africa were armed with two Vickers machine-guns, one mounted in the turret and the other on the left-hand side of the hull. In total a thousand of these were built. Other stop-gap armoured cars included the Edye, Fortress and Susie types, which were assembled in Kenya using civilian vehicle chassis.

To counter the threat from Mussolini in East Africa the British forces in Sudan were increased to 28,000, including a squadron of powerful Matilda tanks from the 4th Royal Tank Regiment. Aosta's forces were swiftly defeated in early 1941. In Eritrea in late January the Italians came under attack from General Platt's 4th and 5th Indian Divisions striking from Sudan and put up a stiff fight. The Italian 4th Colonial Division holding Agordat south-west of Keren was supported by ten medium tanks and a number of L3s. Against this force the 4th Indian Division could muster just four Matilda tanks and a number of carriers to help force the Italian defensive line based on the Laquetat Ridge. Having broken through, they successfully engaged Italian armour beyond Mount Cochen on 31 January 1941. The carriers lured the Italian tanks into a trap and the concealed Matildas attacked them from the rear, knocking out six M11s and five L3s. To attack Keren itself the 4th Indian Division had to manhandle their armoured cars through the Dongolaas Gorge. The Italians managed to hold up Platt's advance until a squadron of Matilda tanks turned the tables at the end of March. The Eritrean capital, Asmara, fell on 1 April, followed by the Italian naval base at Massawa seven days later.

The 1st South African Division and the 11th and 12th African Divisions under General Cunningham, invading from Kenya, successfully occupied Italian Somaliland at the end of February. At Bulo Erillo they captured 141 prisoners and four Italian armoured cars, as well as seizing quantities of fuel at Kismayu and Mogadishu. A small force from Aden retook Berbera on 16 March and joined Cunningham's forces at Jijiga in northern Ethiopia. Addis Ababa, the Ethiopian capital, was liberated on 6 April.

The Duke of Aosta, having lost all his armour, withdrew to Amba Alagi in Ethiopia with 7,000 men and forty guns, but with less than three months of supplies left he surrendered on 19 May 1941. Lingering Italian resistance in Ethiopia was overcome by the end of November. In North Africa the 7th Armoured Division had treated the new South African armoured cars with some scepticism, but in East Africa they served the ad hoc British forces well. The world's attention now switched further north, where the panzers of the Deutsches Afrika Korps were making their presence felt.

During the summer of 1940 Mussolini's forces also attacked Sudan and British Somaliland. Intelligence indicated that his forces had just thirty-five L3s (as seen here) and two dozen M11/39 medium tanks in Abyssinia, and these were used to help drive the weak British forces from Kassala and Berbera. (*Author's Collection*)

To counter Mussolini's overwhelming manpower in East Africa, Churchill conducted a build-up of African (seen here) and South African Divisions in Kenya and Indian Divisions in Sudan. Matilda tanks were also diverted from North Africa. The men pictured here on their troopship are thought to have been photographed by East Africa Command in Mombasa. (*Author's Collection*)

A fighting column headed by a Marmon-Herrington Mk II armoured car; two variants of the South African Mk II were built with differing armament. South Africa had never produced an armoured fighting vehicle before and it was rather a hybrid – the chassis was made by Ford and came from Canada, the Marmon-Herrington four-wheel drive came from America and the armament came from Britain. The armour plate was supplied locally in South Africa and assembly was conducted in old railway workshops. (*Preston Isaac/Basil Lancaster*)

What appears to be a South African Reconnaissance Car Mk I struggling across a river, possibly in Eritrea in 1941. (*Preston Isaac/Basil Lancaster*)

An Italian M11/39 hiding in the scrub. These wholly inadequate tanks were sent to support the Italian 4th Colonial Division at Agordat, but British Matilda tanks easily accounted for six of them. (*Preston Isaac/Basil Lancaster*)

Indian troops in captured Italian positions probably somewhere in Eritrea. The 4th Indian Division was redeployed from North Africa to take part in the East Africa campaign. It was recalled to the Western Desert in March 1941 to take part in Operation Battleaxe, while the 5th Indian Division followed after the Italian surrender in Abyssinia. (*Author's Collection*)

A Fortress armoured car; this type was designed and assembled in Kenya, along with the Edye and Susie armoured cars. Note the very bold camouflage scheme. Like the Marmon-Herrington vehicles, they were a hybrid of bits and pieces. (*Preston Isaac/Basil Lancaster*)

South African troops from the 1st Division at Moyale on the Kenyan–Abyssinian border posing with a trophy of war (an Italian flag) after the Italian forces had hastily withdrawn. From Moyale they struck north into Abyssinia to Yaballo, Shashamanna and on to Addis Ababa. Units also pushed eastward into Italian Somaliland to Kismayu and Mogadishu. (*Author's Collection*)

A First World War vintage Italian Autoblindo Mitragliatrice Lanzia Ansaldo IZ car; although updated in the inter-war years, like most Italian equipment in East Africa it was well past its sell-by date. The IZ armoured car was built by Ansaldo on the Lancia IZ light truck chassis and at the outbreak of the Second World War was still in service with the Italian Army in Libya and East Africa. This particular version has a large cylindrical turret mounting two machine-guns; note the large, single headlight mounted forward on the front of the vehicle. The metal frame over the front of the hull was intended to cut barbed wire, but probably acted as little more than a snag; also it was easily damaged. (*Preston Isaac/Basil Lancaster*)

British troops in East Africa with a modified civilian utility vehicle, possibly a Ford or an International 4×4. The British Army exhibited its usual inventiveness and 'can do' attitude when pressing useful vehicles into service during this campaign. Twin machine-guns appear to be mounted over the cab. (*Preston Isaac/Basil Lancaster*)

East African troops haul a Fortress armoured car up an escarpment prior to an attack on Italian positions. Such armour helped compensate for the lack of tank units during the campaign. (*Preston Isaac/Basil Lancaster*)

A motorised column from the 1st South African Division at Hobok Fort in Abyssinia in 1941. Note the Marmon-Herrington armoured car in the middle of the compound. This is the Mobile Field Force's variant of the Mk II, which was armed with a turret-mounted 7.7mm/0.303-inch Vickers machine-gun. (*Author's Collection*)

A warm Ethiopian welcome for the 'British Aemy': the spelling may have been a little wayward but the sentiment was appreciated. It meant the British could concentrate on the war in North Africa and dispatch the 5th Indian Division north, as much-needed reinforcements. (*Preston Isaac/Basil Lancaster*)

Chapter Five

The Desert Fox Arrives

The first elements of the Deutsches Afrika Korps (DAK) arrived in Tripoli on 14 February 1941 with the disembarkation of the 3rd Reconnaissance Battalion, 5th Light Division; other units, most notably two battalions of the 5th Panzer Regiment, followed. Shortly afterwards the 5th Light Division was renamed the 21st Panzer Division and it, along with the 15th Panzer Division, formed the core of the DAK. The key units were their tank regiments, the 5th Panzer Regiment with the 21st Panzer Division and the 8th Panzer Regiment with the 15th Panzer Division. The ad hoc 90th Light 'Afrika' Division controlled those units not assigned to either of the panzer divisions.

Strictly speaking, the term Afrika Korps applies only to the 15th and 21st Panzer Divisions. All other formations, including the 90th Light Division, the Ramcke Brigade and the Italian armoured and motorised divisions were part of Panzer Armee Afrika. Initially Rommel commanded the latter while Generals Cruewell, Nehring and von Thoma commanded DAK. What is remarkable is that although this force only existed for two years, thanks to its extraordinary operations in the desert it has acquired a certain mystique.

When the 5th Panzer Regiment landed in North Africa it brought with it 150 tanks, including seventy light Panzer Mk IIs; the rest were either Mk IIIs with the L/42 50mm gun or Mk IVs with the L/24 75mm gun. In the face of inevitable battle losses the Panzer Mk IIs were replaced with the two newer models and for much of the campaign there were two Mk IIIs for every Mk II and IV. The 5th and 8th Panzer Regiments also took forty Ausf D and E Mk IVs to North Africa.

The 605th Panzerjäger Battalion, part of the 5th Light Division, also arrived with DAK's first self-propelled gun, the 47mm PaK(t) (Sf) auf PzKpfw I Ausf B (which was a Panzer Mk I chassis fitted with a captured Czech 47mm gun). These vehicles were later supplemented by Marder SP guns utilising Czech tank chassis. The tanks were also supported by assault gun and armoured car units. By March 1941 Rommel had amassed almost 160 panzers supported by sixty Italian tanks in Libya. After his experiences in France Rommel was very familiar with British armour. In fact, following Dunkirk four of the many British tanks captured by Rommel – two Matilda Mk Is and two Mk IIs – had been dispatched to Germany.

Two main anti-tank gun types were deployed by DAK: the 50mm L/42 (and later L/60 PaK 38) and the famous dual-role 88mm flak gun. The excellent 75mm PaK 40 was a later development and did not see service until the closing stages of the campaign. The reputation of the '88' flak gun in North Africa almost reached mythical proportions and it was both feared and respected by the Allies in the Western Desert as no tank could stand up to its killing power. To hold Libya, Rommel dug in his 88s at Sollum and Halfaya and these guns reaped a rich harvest from Churchill's 'Tiger Cubs', which had been rushed straight from Britain's training grounds to the desert battlefield.

Having co-opted Mussolini's armour, Rommel quickly recycled abandoned Italian vehicles and artillery. Italian guns appeared in German positions and reconditioned Italian lorries, cars and motorcycles were soon to be seen on the roads sporting the palm tree and swastika insignia of the Afrika Korps. When General Gariboldi, the Italian Commander-in-Chief North Africa, complained that the equipment was Italian property and should be promptly returned, Rommel expressed a very different opinion. His ally would have no real further say in the prosecution of the war in North Africa.

This gave the impending battle an entirely new complexion. British armour could cope with the Panzer Mk I and Mk II but not the subsequent two models. The Panzer Mk III armed with a 50mm gun was superior to any Allied armour until 1942, and although it had its shortcomings, the Mk IV with its 75mm gun was able to fire armour-piercing, high explosive and smoke shells so it could outshoot British Cruisers and shell exposed 25-pounder gun crews. While the Germans could fire from 3,000 yards (with high explosive), the British tanks would have to wait for them to close to within 1,000–500 yards before they could engage with their solid shot, and in the meantime the artillery would have had to retreat.

War correspondent Alexander Clifford, who covered the 1941 North African campaign, soon became aware of these shortcomings, reporting: 'The Mk IIIs and Mk IVs both had more firepower than anything we had got. We found ourselves up against the Mk III's 50mm guns firing four-and-a-half-pound shells . . . It meant that the British had to start every battle with a sprint of half a mile under fire before they could fire back.' He calculated that to combat the Germans' technological advantage the British would need to start with a 30 per cent superiority in numbers, adding gloomily: 'Of course our military authorities had known and expected it. It was one of the risks they were prepared to take.'

When Rommel struck at Agheila on 24 March 1941, the British 2nd Armoured Division conducted a fighting withdrawal. Losses were not serious but the mechanical reliability of the British tanks was a concern and there were many breakdowns. Then on 2 April Rommel's panzers 'bounced' the Support Group from

Agedabia and a large part of the division was overrun. The 3rd Armoured Brigade was sent to Mechili to cover the withdrawal but by the time Rommel reached Mechili the 3rd Armoured Brigade had little or no fighting capability. The remains of the brigade, short of fuel and with just a dozen tanks left, sped north to Derna, only to be ambushed and destroyed on 6 April.

Rommel's 15th Panzer Division was ready for action by the end of May, meaning that the bulk of those armoured forces facing the 'Tiger Cubs' would be German rather than Italian. The German 5th Light Division was south of Tobruk and the Italian Ariete Division's tanks were on Tobruk's perimeter, along with two Italian infantry divisions.

By late 1941 Rommel had 249 panzers, of which 174 were the more powerful Mk IIIs and IVs, supported by 150 obsolescent Italian M13s of the Ariete Division. Against these, the British could field 765 Cruiser, Matilda and Valentine tanks. Getting reinforcements to Libya meant running the gauntlet of the Royal Navy and the RAF, so obtaining replacement panzers was always something of a problem for the German commanders. For example, after the Battle of Sidi Rezegh in November 1941 the two panzer divisions mustered no more than a hundred tanks between them and on a number of occasions their strength fell even lower.

Despite Rommel's setbacks in late 1941, the Gods of war smiled on him in early January the following year when a convoy berthed in Tripoli carrying seventy-five much-needed panzers and armoured cars. By 20 January his Afrika Korps had 111 combat-ready tanks with another twenty-eight undergoing maintenance; the Italian Motorised Corps had eighty-nine tanks. Even more crucially, ammunition and fuel also arrived so that more than 300 Axis aircraft could be put into the air. The Panzergruppe Afrika was now restructured as the Panzerarmee Afrika, and it included the Ariete Armoured and the Trieste Motorised Divisions. This enabled Rommel to bounce back and go over to the offensive again.

In response to the Matilda, the Germans dispatched the Marder self-propelled anti-tank gun to the 15th Panzer Division, though the units did not arrive until May 1942; it was really the 88mm flak gun that ended the Matilda's reign as 'Queen of the Battlefield'. The Matilda was withdrawn from service in North Africa by the end of July 1942. The British also seemed unable to learn from their mistakes. The Ariete Division and part of the 21st Panzer Division overran the isolated 3rd Motorised Brigade in the spring of 1942 and shortly after the 15th Panzer Division caught the 4th Armoured Brigade on its own and wiped out nearly half its strength.

During June 1942, following Rommel's successful attack on the Gazala Line, he withdrew his armour into the 'Cauldron', in which the three German mobile divisions plus two Italian ones were cut off for a while. Rommel, though, triumphed thanks to his brilliant tactics, especially his anti-tank screen, and forced the British (including the 1st and 32nd Tank Brigades) to retreat from Tobruk. This was a disaster for the British.

Rommel employed superior tactics, training and communications; further, he appreciated the necessity for local superiority and the value of artillery and anti-tank guns. Both were used offensively in support of his panzers rather than as purely defensive weapons. Ironically, in June 1942 Rommel was far more appreciative of General Wavell's efforts than Churchill was, remarking:

> Wavell's strategic planning of the offensive had been excellent. . . . He knew very well the necessity of avoiding any operation which would enable his opponent to fight on interior lines and destroy his formations one by one with locally superior concentrations. But he was put at great disadvantage by the slow speed of his infantry tanks, which prevented him from reacting quickly enough to the moves of our faster vehicles.

A young Afrika Korps private poses in his new uniform in Germany before his deployment to Tripoli. Although Hitler was preparing to invade Russia, Mussolini's military incompetence in North Africa, Albania and Greece (coupled with a coup in Yugoslavia) forced his hand. In early April 1941 Hitler invaded the Balkans and dispatched Rommel to Libya. The diversion of British forces from North Africa to aid the Greeks' short-lived resistance played into Rommel's hands. (*Dr Peter Caddick-Adams*)

Under the codename Operation Sunflower, Hitler's order to assist Mussolini in Libya was given on 6 February 1941. Two days later the first units departed Naples and arrived in Tripoli on 11 February. This DAK parade, put on for the benefit of local Italian military officials, looks very impressive, but little did they realise the true significance of allowing the panzers into Libya. The men are wearing tropical topees, tunics, trousers and long desert boots. (*Dr Peter Caddick-Adams*)

(*Above*) Two Afrika Korps soldiers pose with a local in Tripoli. The young panzer leutnant on the right is wearing early Afrika Korps desert boots, a tropical officer's belt and jodhpurs (soon discarded); he has two ribbons, a tank engagement wound badge and an Iron Cross First Class. He is almost certainly with the 5th Light Division that became the 21st Panzer Division. The NCO on the left (who holds his cigarette cupped in his hand like a veteran) also has two ribbons, an Iron Cross First Class and a wound badge, and also, intriguingly, what looks like a blockade runner's badge (*Abzeichen für Blockadebrecher*). This was instituted on 1 April 1941 and therefore the photo probably dates from April/May 1941; it almost certainly pre-dates July 1941, when the Afrika Korps cuff title was authorised, as neither man is wearing it. (*Dr Peter Caddick-Adams*)

(*Opposite, top*) The advance guard of the 5th Light Division (later the 21st Panzer Division) landed on 14 February 1941 and was rushed up the line to Sirte. The 15th Panzer Division's 8th Panzer Regiment was shipped in three convoys to Libya between 25 April and 6 May 1941. The regiment initially fielded 146 tanks, comprising forty-five Panzer IIs (seen here), seventy-one Panzer IIIs, twenty Panzer IVs and ten command tanks. (*Scott Pick*)

(*Below*) A Panzer III Ausf E from the 21st Panzer Division with the 50mm KwK L/42 gun. The 5th Light Division did not get off to a good start: at Naples a cargo ship caught fire and sank with the loss of ten Panzer Mk IIIs and three Panzer IVs. The replacements for the 5th Panzer Regiment did not reach it until the end of April. (*Author's Collection*)

(*Above*) From early 1941, when DAK's armoured units first arrived, they were equipped with the Panzer Mk IV Ausf C and D and then later with the Ausf E and F1, which were armed with the 75mm KwK L/24 gun, which fired the same high-explosive projectile as the Ausf F2 (dubbed the 'Special' by the British), which was equipped with the L/43. While the Panzer IV was up-gunned with the long-barrelled 75mm L/43 gun to produce the Ausf F2 (seen here in Tunisia), which was capable of penetrating 85mm of armour at 1,000 yards and was superior to the British 6-pounder, its arrival was counter-balanced by the Grant. The F2 was never available in sufficient numbers, with around thirty in each of the panzer divisions at any one time, compared to a hundred Mk IIIs. (*US Army/NARA*)

(*Opposite, top*) This top-heavy self-propelled howitzer consisted of a captured French Lorraine Schlepper or 'Tracteur Blindé' 37L fitted with a German 150mm gun. This conversion, carried out in the summer of 1942, was especially for the benefit of Rommel's forces and examples were issued to the panzer artillery battalion of the 21st Panzer Division. This one was captured in Tunisia. (*US Army/NARA*)

(*Opposite, below*) A side view of the sFH13/1 (Sf) auf Geschützwagen Lorraine Schlepper (f) (Sd Kfz 135/1) showing that the howitzer was really too big for the chassis. In fact, the tractor was unmodified except for a slight strengthening of the suspension. The superstructure was supplied by Alkett and assembly took place in Paris and Krefeld. (*Author's Collection*)

The Panzerjäger 38(t) für 7.62cm Pak(r) was shipped to DAK forces during May–July 1942. They served with the 15th Panzer Division's 33rd and 39th Panzerjäger Battalions, providing a welcome self-propelled, anti-tank gun capability. (*US Army/NARA*)

The smashed remains of a sIG33 auf Fahrgestell Panzerkampfwagen II (Sf) self-propelled 150mm gun knocked out on 27 June 1942 near Mersa Matruh. It consisted of a stretched Panzer II chassis (in order to incorporate the gun) and required an additional road wheel; production was supposed to have commenced in the summer of 1941 but design problems delayed this to the end of the year. In the event only twelve sIG33s were built and shipped to Rommel in early 1942; they served with the 707th and 708th Heavy Infantry Gun Companies until the last were lost the following year. (*Steve Hunnisett/Ron Hunnisett RA*)

Rommel received very few dedicated assault guns such as this Sturmgeschütz Ausf D (in fact he got three), and he was obliged to rely on a hotchpotch of hybrid self-propelled guns mounted on captured Czech and French chassis. It is thought that this particular vehicle may have been photographed in Greece in 1941. (*L.J. Alexander/Corporal Eric Evans RASC*)

This is the Sd Kfz 231 heavy armoured car with drive and steering to all wheels. Although only armed with a 20mm gun and a machine-gun, it conducted vital reconnaissance work for DAK forces in the wastes of the Western Desert. In parts of the desert armoured cars could perform as well or even better than tanks, though on soft sand and steep inclines they were at a disadvantage. (*Author's Collection*)

American troops examine an armoured car support weapon in Sbeitla. The Sd Kfz 233 consisted of the heavy armoured car body fitted with the L/24 short 75mm gun and was intended to give reconnaissance units the ability to engage enemy armour. Although it did not appear until the end of 1942, some were employed along with the Tiger tank in Tunisia. (*US Signal Corps/NARA*)

The 88mm flak 18/36 anti-aircraft gun could also be used in the anti-tank role. The '88' was feared and respected by Allied forces in the Western Desert as no tank could stand up to it. This gun gained an almost mythical reputation and was to reap a rich harvest when Churchill's 'Tiger Cubs' were rushed from Britain's training grounds to the desert battlefield. (*Author's Collection*)

A British Army officer examines a camouflaged anti-tank gun. Rommel's forces became masters in the use of anti-tank guns, which were used offensively to support the panzers rather than solely in a defensive role. Time and time again they brought British armoured attacks to a halt, which then triggered a panzer counter-attack. The Italian technique of using light grey and dirty white colours to camouflage their guns made them virtually invisible at 500 yards. (*NARA*)

The backbone of German medium artillery during the Second World War was the sFH 18 150mm field howitzer developed by Rheinmetall & Krupp in the late 1920s; featuring a split-trail carriage, it had a range of 8.2 miles. This gun is deployed in the Western Desert with its half-track prime mover behind. Note the netting used to camouflage it in an attempt to avoid air attack. (*Australian Army*)

German troops in North Africa hitch a ride on an Sd Kfz 251/7. This half-track was used as a prime mover for artillery, flak and anti-tank guns and was one of the mainstays of the Africa Korps light armoured force. (*US Army/NARA*)

The battered remains of a German Kfz 31 Phänomen Granit 25H field ambulance and an Italian cargo truck. Rommel's forces were forever short of motor transport and regularly made use of captured vehicles or indeed those belonging to the Italian Army. (*US Signal Corps/NARA*)

An Axis convoy under air attack. Note how the road has been built over the dunes. The main coastal road linking Libya and Egypt was regularly strafed and bombed by both sides. The wide-open spaces gave vehicles nowhere to hide and both sides' lines of communication remained vulnerable throughout the war. (*Author's Collection*)

Initially the Luftwaffe's Messerschmitt Bf109s (seen here), Bf110s and Junkers Ju87s and Ju88s inflicted heavy losses on the Desert Air Force as the latter's generally inferior Hawker Hurricanes and Curtiss P-40 Kittyhawks were often flown by inexperienced and under-trained pilots. Once Rommel had rolled the British out of most of Cyrenaica the Me109s and Ju87s were able to support his ground operations flying from Derna and Gazala. By 1942 the Luftwaffe's preference for engaging enemy fighters rather than bombers often left Axis ground forces unsupported, with predictable results. (*Author's Collection*)

However, the Stukas suffered heavy losses attacking Tobruk, forcing Rommel to withdraw a flak regiment that had been countering British armoured attacks. As the war progressed these dive-bombers became increasingly vulnerable. (*Author's Collection*)

The Ju52 transport aircraft provided DAK forces with a vital lifeline throughout the North African campaign. Once established in Cyrenaica, they provided support not only to the Luftwaffe's fighter units but also to Rommel's ground forces. (*Author's Collection/Dr Peter Caddick-Adams*)

The Panzer III was the mainstay of Hitler's early offensives and in use with the Afrika Korps was far superior to any Allied armour before 1942. (*Author's Collection*)

The Tiger tank featured in some of the battles fought in North Africa, but arrived much too late and in too few numbers to be of any help to Rommel fighting in Libya and Egypt. (*Author's Collection*)

A seasoned-looking German NCO (a corporal to judge by his rank chevrons) in Libya wearing the distinctive Bergmütze peaked field cap. This cap was much more popular and more practical than the tropical topee. Uniform colours varied enormously, largely due to the effects of the sun. (*Dr Peter Caddick-Adams*)

Chapter Six

Churchill's 'Battleaxe'

Churchill was furious about the loss of the 3rd Armoured Brigade in early April 1941 and cabled General Wavell demanding to know what had happened. Wavell explained that the units involved were not ready for action and that his Cruiser tanks were appallingly unreliable, stating, '3rd Armoured Brigade practically melted away from mechanical and administrative breakdowns during the retreat, without much fighting, while the unpractised headquarters of the 2nd Armoured Division seems to have lost control.'

Quickly recovering from the shock of Wavell's unwelcome expulsion from Libya, Churchill rallied his forces to secure the defence of Egypt. He ordered that Britain be stripped of every tank and aircraft that could be spared. This was at a time when the country's factories were taking a hammering from the Luftwaffe. Excitedly Churchill wrote to Wavell on 22 April 1941: 'I have been working hard for you in the last few days, and you will, I am sure, be glad to know that we are sending you 307 of our best tanks through the Mediterranean, hoping they will reach you around 10 May. Of these 99 are Cruisers, Mark IV and Mark VI [Crusader I], with necessary spare parts for the latter, and 180 "I" tanks [Matilda].'

The five ships of Churchill's 'Tiger' convoy, escorted by the Royal Navy, passed Gibraltar on 6 May. One ship, the *Empire Song*, was lost with fifty-seven tanks and ten Hurricanes after striking mines in the waters south of Malta, though luckily no one was killed. The rest reached Malta and then pressed on to Alexandria, arriving unscathed on the 12th to deliver 238 much-needed tanks and forty-three Hurricane fighters. While the 'Tiger Cubs' were prepared for action, the British attempted to drive Rommel away from the frontier before the 15th Panzer Division was ready for battle.

Wavell launched Operation Brevity on 15 May 1941. The 22nd Guards Brigade, with twenty-six Matildas, was to capture Fort Capuzzo via Halfaya, while to the south the 2nd Armoured Division's Support Group with twenty-nine old Cruiser tanks was to screen the attack with a push on Sidi Azeiz. The Guards made little headway, losing five Matildas knocked out and thirteen more damaged. Many of the Cruiser tanks broke down on the way to Sidi Azeiz and more broke down on the way back. At Halfaya Pass the 15th Panzer Division captured seven Matilda tanks, three of which were still operational.

By 9 June 1941 all the British tank squadrons had received their new vehicles, but at General Creagh's request they were given another five days' training before the launch of Operation Battleaxe. Later Creagh admitted he was not confident about their chances of victory:

> An answer was difficult since it depended on which side could reinforce the quicker – though we could concentrate on undoubted initial superiority, the Germans could reinforce with their second armoured division from Tobruk, only 80 miles distant, while as far as I knew we had no means of reinforcement at all.

Lieutenant General Sir Noel Beresford-Peirse was placed in command, with the 7th Armoured and 4th Indian Divisions acting as his strike force, though they lacked a brigade each. The 4th Indian Division was to push along the coast through Halfaya towards Sollum and Capuzzo. The 7th Armoured Division comprised the 4th and 7th Armoured Brigades; the former had two regiments (4RTR and 7RTR) equipped with Matildas, while the latter's 2RTR had to make do with inadequate A9, A10 and A13 Cruiser tanks, which although old designs were recently delivered new builds, while 6RTR was issued with Crusaders. Ninety-eight Hurricanes and Tomahawks as well as over a hundred bombers supported the ground forces.

Under Battleaxe, Churchill's ill-prepared 'Tiger Cubs' were thrown recklessly into action on 15 June with the intention of overwhelming Rommel. Lieutenant Colonel Walter O'Carroll, the commander of 4RTR, watched the attack on Halfaya Pass go in:

> The sun was rising behind and light forward was excellent. No guns sounded. The tanks crept on. At Halfaya the month before Major Miles had found the enemy still in bed or shaving when he arrived, but they were Italians. Now it seemed almost too good to be true that the [German] garrison should be so caught again . . .

He was right – it was too good to be true. At 0600 Rommel's 88mm guns opened up. All but one of the thirteen Matildas went up in flames and the attack along the top of the escarpment collapsed. At the bottom of the pass six tanks of A Squadron 4RTR ran into a minefield; four blew up, blocking in the survivors. The attack on the pass ended in a confused shambles. Meanwhile 7RTR reached Capuzzo only to lose five Matildas to German counter-attacks, with another four damaged.

Now it was 2RTR's turn to attack, with 6RTR's Crusaders held back for a surprise blow, but both were bested to the west at Hafid Ridge. Two A9s were lost to German 88mms; equipped only with solid shot, there was nothing they could do against the dug-in anti-tank guns. To the south a flanking attack failed and five tanks were lost after they could not be recalled for lack of radios. The Crusaders were then thrown in and ran straight into a German gun line, losing eleven tanks immediately with another six damaged. Others simply broke down. In the face of over thirty panzers and failing light, the rest withdrew.

By the end of the day only thirty-seven of the hundred Matildas committed to the battle remained operational (although the mechanics had another eleven battleworthy by the following day). It was discovered that the 7th Armoured Brigade had lost half its tanks, while 2RTR had twenty-eight tanks and 6RTR some fifty remaining. Disastrously for Beresford-Peirse, he had lost half his tanks without even bringing Rommel's main panzer force to battle.

Rommel, though, was feeling the pressure. Having lost Capuzzo, he had men isolated at Halfaya, had suffered casualties along Hafid Ridge and lost Point 206. He must have been very reassured by the reports filtering in that the surrounding landscape was littered with knocked-out and broken-down British tanks. Also word came that a panzer battalion from the 5th Light Division had just arrived at Hafid Ridge and the rest of the division was en route. Similarly the 15th Panzer Division had yet to fully commit itself to the fight, its artillery and anti-tank units having borne the brunt of most of the British attack. Those panzers involved around Capuzzo had been used solely to lure the 'Tiger Cubs' on to the waiting anti-tank guns.

Lieutenant Heinz Werner Schmidt accompanied Rommel to view the battle:

> It was bonny fighting that we saw. Wavell's tanks broke into a number of infantry positions, despite the intensive fire of our 88mm guns, which they had scarcely expected to meet. The crews manning the 88s sat high up and unprotected at their sights. When one man fell, another of the crew took his place. . . . despite the heavy losses caused by the artillery, the British infantry with rare gallantry pressed forward across the Halfaya wadis.

By the afternoon of the 16th 6RTR had withdrawn to the frontier with just ten operational Crusaders. The Panzers launched another attack at 1900 and rolled over 6RTR and 2RTR; only the onset of darkness saved them from complete annihilation. The following day Rommel massed his panzers and struck west of Sidi Suleiman, reaching the town at 0600; the Matildas withdrew from their exposed position at Capuzzo, and a six-hour battle followed. Battleaxe had been stopped in its tracks and the Germans were left in possession of the battlefield. Rommel commented, 'Great numbers of destroyed British tanks littered the country through which the two divisions had passed.' He went on to observe:

> Thus the three-day battle of Sollum was over. It had finished with a complete victory for the defence, although we might have dealt the enemy far greater damage than we actually had done. The British had lost, in all, over 200 tanks and their casualties in men had been tremendous. We, on the other hand, had lost about twenty-five tanks totally destroyed.

In fact, according to British figures sixty-four Matildas were lost, along with twenty-seven Cruiser tanks, though more Crusaders fell into German hands as a result of mechanical troubles than through battle damage. Although the Crusader was under-gunned, Rommel was quite impressed by it, noting: 'Had this tank been equipped with a heavier gun, it could have made things extremely unpleasant for us.'

The previous successes of Wavell and O'Connor had been swept away. Churchill by his own admission was disconsolate at the failure of Battleaxe: 'Although this action may seem small compared with the scale of the Mediterranean in all its various campaigns, its failure was to me a most bitter blow. Success in the Desert would have meant the destruction of Rommel's audacious force.'

On the 21st Wavell fell on his sword and signalled Churchill, 'Am very sorry for the failure of Battleaxe and the loss of so many Tiger Cubs, ... I was over-optimistic and should have advised you that 7th Armoured Division required more training before going into battle.... but ... I was impressed by the apparent need for immediate action.'

By March 1941 Rommel had 160 panzers in Libya, including the Panzer Mk III armed with the KwK L/42 50mm gun. This was superior to any Allied armour until 1942. Along with the Panzer IV, the Panzer III Ausf J and Ausf M comprised DAK's main armoured striking power. (*NARA*)

A moment of relaxation next to the Mediterranean Sea for this German tank crew. The Panzer Mk II served Rommel's armoured units in a reconnaissance role. (*Author's Collection*)

The Germans liked British carriers and after being captured in North Africa large numbers of them were pressed back into service as the Gepanzerter Maschinengewehr Trager Bren 731(e). For example, Rommel captured fifty Bren Carriers at El Agheila on 24 March 1941. The Germans found them superior to the French Chenillettes; the Luftwaffe also used Bren Carriers, as they did the Chenillettes, for towing tasks. (*Author's Collection*)

Churchill was determined to do everything he could to stop Rommel and he stripped Britain of every available tank and shipped them to Egypt in what was dubbed the 'Tiger' convoy. (*Author's Collection*)

British Matilda IIs being loaded for shipment. This tank had already proved itself against the Italians and the 'Tiger' convoy included almost 200. Note how the wartime censor has blanked out the horizon. (*Author's Collection*)

Miraculously the 'Tiger' convoy lost only one ship during its perilous journey from England to Egypt. The *Empire Song* struck a mine south of Malta, and went down with fifty-seven precious tanks and ten Hurricane fighters. (*Author's Collection*)

The 'Tiger' convoy reached the British-held island of Malta on 9 May 1941 and arrived in Alexandria three days later carrying 238 tanks and forty-three fighters. In the meantime Rommel's Deutsches Afrika Korps had rolled the British out of Cyrenaica, destroying the 3rd Armoured Brigade in the process. (*Author's Collection*)

British troops at roll call. The arrival of new equipment greatly raised morale but Churchill's insistence on throwing it into battle as quickly as possible was soon to cause problems. The type of sun helmet these men are wearing was soon dispensed with, and was particularly unpopular with tank crews. (*Author's Collection*)

A British column moves up for the attack. Motor transport was notoriously vulnerable to air attack: the open landscape and the dust thrown up by the wheels meant vehicles were easy to spot. (*L.J. Alexander/Corporal Eric Evans RASC*)

A British convoy comes under attack from German aircraft or artillery. (*Author's Collection*)

New Zealander motor transport somewhere in the Western Desert – such lorries had to perform in a wide range of climatic conditions. (*Author's Collection*)

A British 25-pounder gun engaging enemy targets. Although designed as an artillery piece, it was also used in an anti-tank role against Rommel's panzers. (*Author's Collection*)

German heavy artillery firing in support of the panzers. German gunners constantly supported the tank battles rather than waiting for the fight to come to them. (*NARA*)

The mechanical unreliability of the new Cruiser tank, the Mk VI Crusader (A14), meant it performed badly during Battleaxe; in fact more broke down than were lost to enemy action. The design was rushed and there were insufficient development trials, but to be fair to the designers there was a war on. This one has clearly been knocked out by Rommel's anti-tank guns. (*Author's Collection*)

German troops pose on their prize, a captured Matilda tank, numbers of which were lost during Operations Brevity and Battleaxe in May and June 1941 respectively. By the end of the first day of Battleaxe, only thirty-seven of the hundred Matildas committed to the fight were operational. (*Dr Peter Caddick-Adams*)

Another victim – in just three days Rommel stopped the British attack in its tracks, claiming 200 enemy tanks destroyed. The actual figure for tanks destroyed was less than half this, but included sixty-four Matildas, such as this one. (*Dr Peter Caddick-Adams*)

A posed shot of British infantry taking a Panzer III's crew prisoner. Of interest is the clutter on the outside of the tank, especially the numerous spare water bottles dangling from the turret storage bin and the rack of 'Jerry' cans at the front. (*Author's Collection*)

While far from rare, this photograph of Rommel reconnoitring with the 15th Panzer Division has been included because of what is to his left. This is a Leichte Panzerspähwagen (fu) Sd Kfz 223, essentially a light armoured car fitted with a long-range radio. The raised square aerial frame is just visible. (*NARA*)

Chapter Seven

Crusader – Panzergruppe Afrika Driven Back

In late August Churchill, still smarting about the very public failure of his 'Tiger Cubs', wrote to his Minister of Supply and the Chief of the Imperial General Staff in a state of irritation:

> We ought to try sometimes to look ahead. The Germans turned up in Libya with 6-pounder guns in their tanks, yet I suppose it would have been reasonable for us to have imagined they would do something to break up the ordinary 'I' tank. This had baffled the Italians at Bardia, etc. The Germans had specimens of it in their possession taken at Dunkirk, also some Cruiser tanks, so it was not difficult for them to prepare weapons which would defeat our tanks.

The 'Tiger' convoy had stretched Britain's resources to the limit and by early July 1941, for the defence of the British Isles, Churchill could muster 1,141 infantry and Cruiser tanks, of which just 391 were considered fit for action. British repair facilities at this stage remained lamentable and a month later 25 per cent of the infantry tanks were still out of action, as were 157 of the 400 Cruiser tanks. Despite the success of the 'Tiger' convoy, the Royal Navy believed the Mediterranean was becoming too dangerous and so escorted the next convoy, of another fifty Cruiser and fifty infantry tanks, around the Cape, but they did not reach Suez until mid-July.

When Panzergruppe Afrika was established, consisting of the 15th and 21st Panzer Divisions, they were equipped with about 170 Panzer Mks II, III and IV, as well as a dozen British Matildas and seventeen Valentines. Rommel's 'Tiger Cubs' went into action with the 21st Panzer Division on 14 September 1941, when three columns pushed into Egypt.

By November the Eighth Army had come into being, and a second generation of British infantry and Cruiser tanks, along with the American Stuart light tank, had reached North Africa. The production runs for Britain's early Cruiser tanks was fairly limited (125 A9s, 175 A10s and 335 A13s) and all were withdrawn from service in late 1941, having been replaced by the Crusader and Stuart. The British massed 756 tanks, mostly Matildas and Valentines, for Operation Crusader. They enjoyed mixed success when the operation was launched on 20 November employing two whole corps, 13 Corps (1st Army Tank Brigade, plus the 2nd New Zealand and 4th Indian Divisions) and 30 Corps (the 7th Armoured and 1st South African Divisions, plus the 22nd Guards Brigade).

The intention for Crusader was for 13 Corps to bypass the Axis frontier defences to the south and attack along the Via Balbia towards Tobruk. To the south 30 Corps was to advance north-westward across the desert, smash the enemy's panzers in the area of Sidi Rezegh airfield and then link up with the Tobruk garrison, which was to break out in the Belhamed–El Duda area. The powerful 7th Armoured Division consisted of three armoured brigades: the 4th armed with the newly arrived American M3 Stuarts, and the 7th and 22nd both equipped with British Cruiser tanks. The Tobruk garrison included the 32nd Army Tank Brigade, which comprised four Matilda squadrons and a regiment of Cruisers and light tanks.

Major-General F.W. von Mellenthin recalled,

> To meet this attack the Panzergruppe had 249 German and 146 Italian tanks. . . . Of the German tanks, 70 were Mark IIs, which only mounted a heavy machine gun, and could therefore play no part in the tank battle, except as reconnaissance vehicles. The bulk of our strength consisted of 35 Mk IVs and 139 Mk IIIs; we also had five British Matildas, of which we thought highly.

Once more, however, the British tanks were lured into a trap sprung by concealed armour and anti-tank guns, and the attack quickly came unstuck. Nonetheless, the British held on and Rommel, with his two panzer and single Italian armoured divisions over-extended, was forced to retreat. During these engagements Rommel's 'Tiger Cubs' caused confusion on both sides.

Leutnant Schmidt of the 15th Panzer Division was involved in the capture of a British tank recovery vehicle in November 1941 near Sidi Azeiz. Afterwards, heading south towards Maddalena, he was alarmed to be informed that he had British tanks behind him. Three anti-tank guns were set up to block the twelve advancing Matildas; two were destroyed and the rest fanned out. Schmidt and his gunners were in danger of being surrounded and were considering retreating when two more Matildas came up behind them. Schmidt takes up the story:

> I glanced back with a vague idea of withdrawal if that were possible amid this fire. To my horror I saw two more British Mark IIs moving towards us. Then to my gasping relief I recognised swastika markings on them: they were two of the British tanks that had been captured at Halfaya during 'Battleaxe' months before.

When the German commander surrendered at Bardia, some 9,000 German and Italian troops were taken prisoner. A total of 4,000 Germans and 10,000 Italians were captured at Bardia, Sollum and Halfaya. The campaign also cost them about 300 tanks, while the British lost 278.

Since Bardia was one of Rommel's major supply bases, perhaps the worst aspect of the disaster for him was the loss of vast quantities of supplies, guns and ammunition. This was an irreplaceable loss from which, despite his subsequent victories in 1942, he never really recovered. Rommel attempted not to repeat the same mistake at the end of the year when he sought to evacuate at least part of the 10,000 tons of Axis material at Tobruk but British air raids destroyed 2,000 tons of precious fuel at Benghazi. Likewise, when Rommel was forced out of Tripoli in early 1943, he managed to spirit away almost all of his supplies – quite remarkably, most of it was moved by road.

Italian bombers attacked Malta in the summer of 1940, violently at first but soon with diminishing strength. The Luftwaffe's first limited offensive against the island in the spring of 1941 had the basic objective of holding Maltese defences down while DAK forces were ferried across from Italy. Once the German II Air Corps had moved to Sicily, life on the island became much more difficult. Attacks began in December 1941 and reached their height in April 1942. In the meantime more British tanks were shipped round the Cape and via the Suez Canal rather than risk the Mediterranean again. (*Author's Collection*)

Maltese workers cutting air raid shelters in the island's soft sandstone. During the summer of 1941 the island was given the chance to recuperate. Of the three large supply convoys totalling thirty-nine transports that reached Malta that year only one ship was lost. Air Vice Marshal H.P. Lloyd, who took over command of the RAF units there in May, is said to have remarked, 'You wouldn't have known there was a war on.' The RAF and Royal Navy were not idle, though, successfully attacking Axis shipping and Rommel's forces suffered accordingly. (*Author's Collection*)

After the initial engagements in North Africa these Germans had every reason to look and feel confident. Operation Crusader, though, would soon put a dent in their morale. Note their mixture of sun helmets and field caps. (*Dr Peter Caddick-Adams*)

To fend off Operation Crusader, Rommel could muster 139 Panzer IIIs. This particular one with the L/42 gun has a British Daimler scout car parked in front of it. By the end of 1941 Axis forces had lost 300 tanks and the British a similar number, but they had retaken Bardia, Sollum and Halfaya. (*Author's Collection*)

A German NCO poses by his 4x4 staff car, in this case a Horch Kfz 15. He is kitted out with long desert boots and what seems to be a sage green uniform. The palm tree/swastika insignia of the Afrika Korps is clearly visible on the driver's door. In the second shot another soldier does his laundry next to a similar vehicle; again the DAK symbol can be seen quite clearly. (*Dr Peter Caddick-Adams*)

Two of Rommel's 'Tiger Cubs'; after Battleaxe, the Germans re-employed limited numbers of captured British Matilda (seen here) and Crusader tanks. (*Author's Collection*)

The Crusader proved a great disappointment for British tank crews, but nonetheless went into battle again during Operation Crusader and continued in service until the very end of the war in North Africa. (*Author's Collection*)

Although the Valentine went into production in 1940, it first joined the Eighth Army's tank brigades in June 1941 and played a key role in Operation Crusader. It subsequently played an important part in the desert fighting, but, like the Crusader, it was armed with the inadequate 2-pounder anti-tank gun. In contrast, the Valentine did gain a reputation for reliability (it is reported that after El Alamein some drove over 3,000 miles on their own tracks). (*Author's Collection*)

A welcome addition to the British tank inventory was the American-supplied M3 Stuart light tank. The first eighty-four arrived in Egypt in July 1941 and by November this number had risen to 163. While it was under-gunned (it had a 37mm gun) and poorly armoured, it was reliable and very mobile in a reconnaissance role. It, too, was blooded during Operation Crusader. (*Author's Collection*)

German troops take a meal in front of an Italian M13/40. Rommel remained reliant on the Italians' contribution to his tank force (the type of Mautlier half-track indicates that this photo was probably taken in Italy or the Balkans). (*Author's Collection*)

The crew of a Crusader seem to be examining their handiwork – a blazing Panzer Mk IV destroyed during Operation Crusader. It is unlikely, however, that the Crusader knocked it out with its 2-pounder gun. The open turret hatch indicates that at least some of the crew managed to bale out before the flames took hold. (*Author's Collection*)

Australian troops plunder a broken-down M13/40. The Italians were able to field a single armoured division with 146 tanks at the time of Operation Crusader. Axis forces became over-extended and had little choice but to retreat in the face of the determined British offensive. (*Australian Army*)

A captured German 150mm Lorraine Schlepper self-propelled howitzer on its low-loader. Fewer than a hundred of these were produced and about half of them ended up in North Africa. While the gun was welcome, the fighting compartment was cramped and the superstructure offered an alarmingly high silhouette for enemy gunners. Many of those photographed seem to have been abandoned, raising a question over their mechanical reliability. (*Author's Collection*)

The Desert Air Force hurried Rommel on his way. The specks are his motor transport vehicles scattering across the Western Desert as they try desperately to escape the bursting bombs dropped by attacking light bombers. (*Author's Collection*)

These abandoned Me109s were captured when British forces overran Axis airfields. Often the aircraft were already unairworthy and had been cannibalised for spares, as seems to be the case with the second aircraft. (*Author's Collection*)

An abandoned German 210mm heavy field gun. Although very accurate, its weight greatly reduced its mobility, meaning it was not something that could be withdrawn in a hurry. Artillery Command 104, equipped with heavy siege guns, was established by Rommel to reduce Tobruk's defences in 1942; its inventory included eighty-four Italian 149mm guns, thirty-six Italian 105mms, forty French 150mms and twelve French 100mms. (*Author's Collection*)

Chapter Eight

Grant and Sherman – The Americans Are Coming!

America supplied the Eighth Army with three main types of tank, the M3 Stuart light tank and the M3 Lee/Grant and M4 Sherman medium tanks. While the Sherman became the single most important tank in the British inventory by virtue of its vast numbers, it was the Grant that arrived in the nick of time to save the Eighth Army in North Africa. The Germans first came up against American-built armour fighting with the British Army in Egypt and Libya and subsequently with the US Army in Tunisia. The very first Stuarts were delivered in July 1941 and were used to replace British-built light tanks; they were followed by the Grant (the introduction of the American Lend-Lease Act in March 1941 also enabled Britain to receive numbers of the slightly differently armed Lee).

After the British Army's escape from Dunkirk and the loss of virtually all its equipment, a British Tank Commission was dispatched to Washington in June 1940 with a view to both getting British tanks built in America and procuring American tanks. In the event they ordered 500 M3 medium tanks dubbed the Grant by the British in honour of General Ulysses S. Grant. The first 200 were shipped to the Eighth Army in early 1942. For the coming Gazala battle the 4th Armoured Brigade was equipped with 167 Grants, giving them at last a tank with superior firepower to any German armoured fighting vehicle. By June 1942 a further 250 M3s had been successfully shipped to Egypt along with American instructors.

Following Rommel's capture of Tobruk that very month, President Roosevelt proposed sending the US 2nd Armored Division to help, but as it would take up to five months to get them there it was decided to dispatch their Sherman tanks instead. Around 300 M4 Shermans, mainly the cast-hull M4A1 variant, were shipped to the Eighth Army by October 1942, along with a hundred new M7 self-propelled howitzers. Washington generously made good convoy losses by withdrawing further tanks issued to American units. Elements of the 2nd Armoured Brigade (1st Armoured Division), the 8th and 24th Armoured Brigades (10th Armoured Division) and the 9th Armoured Brigade (2nd New Zealand Division) were issued with the M4A1s. While the Sherman was easily superior to the obsolescent British Cruisers, they caught fire very easily and the British crews soon nicknamed them 'Ronsons' after the lighter, while the Germans called them 'Tommy Cookers'.

The American-built Grant met with general approval; it was reasonably fast (unlike the Matilda), reliable (unlike the Crusader) and its 75mm gun could take on German armour and anti-tank crews on a more equal footing. The only problem was that the gun was mounted on the right side of the hull, thereby greatly restricting its arc of fire. The Grants first went into action in North Africa in May 1942 at Gazala, where their 75mm guns gave the Germans a nasty shock. 'Up to May of 1942 our tanks had in general been superior in quality to corresponding British types,' noted Rommel in his diary. 'This was now no longer true, at least not to the same extent.' He added, 'The advent of the new American tank had torn great holes in our ranks. Our entire force now stood in heavy and destructive combat with a superior enemy.'

Rommel struck back, seizing Tobruk on 21 June 1942 and capturing about fifty tanks from the dispirited garrison. By the time he had captured Tobruk, his forces had taken or destroyed over a thousand armoured fighting vehicles and almost 400 guns, as well as seizing 45,000 prisoners. Rommel's reward was elevation to field marshal. However, by October 1942 some 600 Grants had arrived in Egypt.

While the concept of the M3 was good, it was only really an interim fix and both the Grant and Lee tank types were replaced as the M4 Sherman became available. The first Shermans lost to German mines and anti-tank guns were those of the British 9th Armoured Brigade during the opening stages of the Battle of El Alamein on 23 October 1942. The first tank-to-tank engagement took place the following day between Shermans of the 2nd Armoured Brigade and tanks of Rommel's 15th Panzer Division.

Rommel was equally impressed by the Sherman: 'Their new tank, the General Sherman, which came into action for the first time during this battle [El Alamein], showed itself to be far superior to ours.' Understandably he was not happy about this development. Indeed, the turning point for Rommel had come – by this stage his forces were completely outnumbered in terms of both manpower and equipment. Crucially Montgomery's Eighth Army had 170 Grants, 252 Shermans, 294 Crusaders, 119 Stuarts and 194 Valentines ready for its knock-out blow. Four British Churchill tanks were also present at El Alamein. After fierce fighting, Rommel was thrown back with the loss of over 400 irreplaceable panzers. Montgomery lost half his tank force but some 350 were repairable.

American-built armour first went into action with the American Army against the Vichy French in North Africa. When American units were deployed overseas, they normally exchanged their medium M3s for M4s, and the only unit not to do this was the US 1st Armored Division. This unit formed part of the Centre Task Force of Operation Torch during the landings in Algeria on 7–8 November 1942. Although Shermans replaced the 1st Armored Division's battle casualties, M3s remained on its strength throughout the campaign. The Sherman first went into action with the Americans in Tunisia in January 1943.

Armour enhancements were not all one-sided. During early 1942 Rommel was supplied with the Panzer Mk III Ausf J armed with the long-barrelled KwK39 L/60 50mm gun which proved very useful against the Grant and the Valentine. Adolf Hitler initially wanted the L/60 installed in the Mk III in the summer of 1940 and was not pleased to see the initial Ausf J armed with the shorter L/42 gun when it went into production in 1941. While this variant ended up armed with either the L/42 or L/60, all subsequent Mk III Ausf L and M were fitted with the longer gun. From April 1942 spaced armour 20mm thick was also fitted to the gun mantlet and hull front, including on those deployed to North Africa.

The most common Panzer Mk IVs were the Ausf D, E and F1, which made up around 25 per cent of Rommel's armoured formations. They were armed with the short 75mm KwK37 L/24 anti-tank gun, which was inferior to the later 50mm gun of the Panzer IIIs. In the summer of 1942 Rommel began to receive the up-gunned F2 armed with the long-barrelled 75mm KwK40 L/43 gun; this could penetrate 85mm of armour at 1,000 yards and was superior to both the British 6-pounder and the Grant's 75mm gun, which could only pierce 45mm of armour at 1,000 yards.

At the same time Rommel also received the Panzerjäger 38(t), which married captured Russian 76.2mm anti-tank guns with Czech-manufactured 38(t) tank chassis, and the Geschützwagen Lorraine Schlepper (f), which comprised a tracked French artillery tractor mounting a German 150mm howitzer. None of these vehicles was supplied in any significant numbers.

Similarly Rommel received just three Sturmgeschütz Ausf D assault guns (armed with the short 75mm gun) and just twelve sIG33s (which mounted a 150mm field gun on a stretched Panzer Mk II chassis) during 1942. The Tiger I, with the powerful KwK36 L/56 88mm anti-tank gun did not arrive until the following year, by which time the Allies were already well aware of its capabilities following its performance on the Eastern Front. By mid-1942 Rommel increasingly lacked adequate armoured fighting vehicles, supplies and reinforcements in the face of ever-growing numbers of American-supplied tanks.

The M3 General Stuart light tank was the first American tank to be supplied to the Eighth Army. Simply known as the Stuart, its British crews also affectionately dubbed it the 'Honey'. (*US Army/NARA*)

This frontal shot of the American M3 General Lee (identifiable by the machine-gun cupola on the turret) shows how limited its sponson-mounted 75mm gun was, with only a 30-degree traverse. Despite this, it was to play a significant role at El Alamein. (*US Army/NARA*)

A British tank crew restock their Grant's ammunition. It was an unusual design, with a 37mm gun in the turret and a 75mm gun mounted on the right-hand side of the hull. (*Author's Collection*)

A Grant passes a burning Panzer Mk I on 6 June 1942, during the Gazala fighting. By October 1942 nearly 600 M3 Grant/Lee tanks had been delivered to the British in North Africa. Ultimately there was little Rommel could do against such decisive numbers. (*Author's Collection*)

A British Sherman, which appears to be the cast-hull M4A1 type, takes on ammo during a lull in the fighting. The British Eighth Army had received about 270 Shermans by October 1942. Churchill claimed that he had 'gone on his knees' to persuade President Roosevelt to send these tanks and then complained bitterly when he was informed they could not go into battle immediately. (*Author's Collection*)

Smiling American tank crew undergoing training on the Sherman at Fort Knox, Kentucky. Plans to send a US armoured division to help in Egypt were not practical so the tanks were sent instead. (*US Army/NARA*)

With the Sherman tank came the Howitzer Motor Carriage M7 known as the Priest. Combining the chassis of the M3 medium tank and a 105mm howitzer, it provided much-needed self-propelled artillery. Once again they were diverted from production intended for American troops. (*US Army/NARA*)

Grant tanks plough their way through the mud and rain in Tunisia. After the campaign those remaining were sent to the Far East to fight the Japanese. (*Author's Collection*)

A series of photos taken of three different M3 Lee crews serving with the 2nd Battalion, 12th Armored Regiment, 1st Armored Division, at Souk el Arba in Tunisia. The men seem in good cheer though it was their M3s rather than the Shermans that bore the brunt of the initial fighting following the Allied landings in French North Africa. (*US Signal Corps/NARA*)

American troops bringing ashore an M7 self-propelled gun in North Africa. (*US Army/NARA*)

American air crews being congratulated by Major General Russell L. Maxwell USAAF in front of a British Grant. Maxwell commanded the USAAF detachment deployed to Egypt in the summer of 1942 to fly in support of the RAF. This ensured that American bombers as well as tanks fought with the Eighth Army. (*Author's Collection*)

A British Sherman M4 A2 or A4 (with the three-piece bolted nose casting) taking part in a landing exercise involving a Landing Craft Tank in North Africa prior to the invasion of Sicily on 10 July 1943. The lack of such craft greatly hindered the Allied landings in French North Africa and meant that the medium tanks had to be landed at the quayside. (*Author's Collection*)

Starting life with a 37mm gun, the Panzer Mk III received successive improvements, of which the version depicted here was the ultimate in Afrika Korps service. The long-barrelled L/60 50mm gun achieved velocities of up to 3,930 feet per second, enabling it to engage most British tanks with success beyond 1,000 yards. It did not, though, become available until early 1942. (*NARA*)

By August 1942 Rommel had received only twenty-seven Panzer Mk IV F2s armed with the longer L/43 gun, which he employed to spearhead his offensives since its gun could penetrate all British and American armour at a distance. While more of these panzers arrived between August and October 1942, they could not match the quantities of tanks reaching the Eighth Army. (*Author's Collection*)

The Panzer IV F2 was a good tank but it was never available in North Africa in decisive numbers. This appears to be the follow-up Ausf G fitted with the new muzzle brake, which went into production in May 1942. This model is in Tunisia, as the Schürzen armour on the turret was not introduced until 1943. (*Author's Collection*)

The Panzerjäger 38(t) für 7.62cm Pak(r) also arrived in North Africa in the summer of 1942 providing a useful self-propelled anti-tank gun capability in the face of the Grant. (*Australian Army*)

A column of British 'Honey' light tanks passing a burnt-out Panzer Mk III. In the foreground is a Sturmgeschütz or assault gun; in early 1942 *Sonderverband* (Detachment for Special Employment) 288 took three Ausf D to Africa, seeing action at Gazala and Tobruk. (*US Army/NARA*)

German efforts to strength DAK forces were too little too late. In December 1942, following the Allied landings in French North Africa, the 10th Panzer Division was shipped from southern France to Tunisia. This knocked-out Panzer III belonged to the division's 7th Panzer Regiment. (*NARA*)

The Tiger I represented the most powerful panzer deployed to North Africa. Elements of two battalions were shipped to Tunisia from Sicily, but they were insufficient in number to have any great impact on the fighting. (*Author's Collection*)

A US M2 half-track (the M3/M5 personnel carrier had a slightly longer hull) photographed at Oran, Algeria, in early April 1943. The first production M2s, designed for reconnaissance and as prime movers for artillery, were delivered to the American Army in May 1941. (*US Army/NARA*)

Chapter Nine

El Alamein – Rommel Defeated

General Claude Auchinleck replaced General Ritchie in the summer of 1942; soon realising that holding western Egypt was not possible, he prepared a mobile defence in depth between Mersa Matruh and El Alamein. The latter offered the only defensive line in North Africa that cannot be outflanked, due to the 700-ft cliffs of the Qattara Depression just 40 miles to the south, and the Eighth Army fortified this gap. While Rommel was aiming to push his panzers all the way through to Alexandria, Cairo and the Suez Canal, Auchinleck in turn planned to stop him and break through to the west. Rommel was handicapped by a supply line that trailed back as far as Tripoli.

Rommel's initial capture of Mersa Matruh led to the first Battle of Alamein, though by this stage his armoured forces were reduced to about a dozen tanks. Rommel spent two weeks trying to dislodge the British, who then in turn spent two weeks trying to drive back the Germans. This series of engagements lasted twenty-seven days and commenced on 1 July 1942. The Ruweisat Ridge was the scene of especially heavy fighting. While the New Zealanders and Indians drove the Italians from their positions on 14 July, they bypassed the 8th Panzer Regiment.

The following day there was no sign of the 22nd Armoured Brigade, which was supposed to support the New Zealanders. Predictably the panzers counter-attacked, catching the New Zealanders on three sides, and their advance was only checked by the belated appearance of the British tanks. The two sides fought each other to a standstill and the battle had tailed off by 27 July; Axis losses amounted to 22,000 men and 100 tanks, while the British lost 13,000 men and 193 tanks.

Unfortunately Auchinleck's decision to give ground and his failure to defeat Rommel decisively cost him his job. By this stage the Afrika Korps' situation was so dire – lacking panzers, exhausted and under-strength – that a British victory was largely assured. Montgomery arrived to take command of the Eighth Army's gathering strength on 13 August 1942. Despite his enemy's numerical superiority, Rommel, with typical flair, sought to catch Monty off-balance by attacking first.

Due to refuelling problems and the slowness of the Italian Ariete and Trieste Divisions in getting through the British defences, Rommel was unable to strike Alam Halfa until 31 August. Nonetheless, when his new Panzer Mk IVs with their high-velocity 75mm guns supported by Stuka dive-bombers did attack, they caused heavy losses among the dug-in British Grant tanks. Times had changed, though, and things did not go to plan for Rommel as his attack became bogged down. For the first time the British also had substantial numbers of 6-pounder anti-tank guns. Under attack from the RAF, Rommel's forces had little choice but to withdraw to their original start line.

Montgomery, never a man to rush headlong into anything, did not give chase, but instead chose to bide his time while gathering even greater strength ready for a decisive knock-out blow. Before Alamein, Montgomery tricked Rommel into believing that he had an extra armoured division by employing a complete divisional HQ (from the 8th Armoured Division) using radio traffic to create the impression that it was controlling the arrival of this new unit. In reality, it had no tanks at all. Montgomery, though, went into battle with a superiority of about 2:1 in troops and 1,100 tanks to Rommel's 500 (of which 300 were of an inferior type). On top of this, Montgomery had almost 1,000 field guns, 800 6-pounder and 500 2-pounder anti-tank guns. On 23 October 1942 a massive British artillery bombardment heralded the second battle of El Alamein.

Montgomery had finally learned that it was not wise to throw his tanks against Rommel's gun line so he directed his infantry to first breach the enemy minefields. Once two safe corridors had been secured, he planned to push through the 1st and 10th Armoured Divisions to Tel el Aqqaqir to prepare for an enemy counter-attack. Near the Qattara Depression in the far south the 7th Armoured Division launched a diversionary attack with the intention of pinning down Rommel's reserves, most notably the 21st Panzer Division. While Monty's infantry engaged the Axis defences, his armour, despite its overwhelming numbers, was at first unable to break through. The battle turned into a slugging match that Rommel simply could not win.

Rommel could clearly see the writing on the wall for the Axis cause in North Africa. This battle is 'turning the tide of war in Africa against us,' Rommel wrote, 'and, in fact, probably representing the turning point of the whole vast struggle. The conditions under which my gallant troops entered the battle were so disheartening that there was practically no hope of our coming out of it victorious.'

By 26 October Major General R. Brigg's 1st Armoured Division had reached Kidney Ridge and was threatening to cut the Axis main north–south line of communication along the Rahman Track. The 2nd Rifle Brigade was sent forward to set up Outpost Snipe and came into contact with the 15th Panzer Division and the Italian Littorio Armoured Division. Although only of battalion strength, the 2nd Rifle

Brigade fortunately had almost twenty 6-pounder anti-tank guns and was able to drive off the enemy attacks. The 21st Panzer Division then found itself caught between the anti-tank guns and the rest of the 1st Armoured Division. Subsequently the battlefield around the Snipe position was littered with twenty-one panzers, eleven Italian tanks and five tank destroyers; it was also believed that another twenty tanks had been knocked out but recovered by the Axis forces.

On 27 October Montgomery reorganised his forces and despite mounting losses maintained his pressure in the northern sector of the battle. Rommel was in an unenviable position: despite all his skills, by the end of October he knew the British had still not committed the bulk of their 800 tanks, against which he could pit just ninety panzers and 140 Italian tanks. Then, on 1 November, Operation Supercharge finally overwhelmed the exhausted Axis troops.

Rommel's men suffered the impact of Montgomery's long-expected major attack that night. South-west of Hill 28 the British broke through the 15th Panzer Division's front; captured documents showed the Germans were now facing up to 500 tanks, which drove west and overran a unit from the Trieste Armoured Division. To Rommel's dismay, his observers reported another 400 British tanks waiting east of the minefields. By the evening of 2 November Rommel had just thirty-five serviceable panzers; by the 4th this figure had fallen to just twenty.

Despite the British armour's breakthrough on the 4th, the Germans were already retiring back towards Libya. The British pursuit was delayed because of Montgomery's caution, bad weather and fuel shortages. Rommel's remaining troops – the equivalent of two divisions from his original dozen – rumbled back along the coast road harried by the Desert Air Force as they went. This was no rout, and Rommel turned to fight at every possible defensive position. Montgomery, instead of throwing everything he had at Rommel, kept trying to outflank him and as a result, the retreating Axis forces kept slipping through the net.

Fuel supplies became an increasing problem for Rommel, not only in getting it shipped to Tripoli but also in transporting it to the front. After the defeat at Alamein, the 21st Panzer Division was almost completely immobilised south-west of Quasaba for the want of fuel; only the timely arrival of the Voss Group prevented the division being overrun. Nonetheless the 21st Panzer Division was forced to destroy all but four of its remaining thirty tanks and to withdraw westward in its surviving wheeled transport.

The arrival of the British 6-pounder (57mm) anti-tank gun in early 1942 provided a much-needed upgrade to the Eighth Army's anti-tank capabilities. It began to replace the obsolete 2-pounder (40mm) and allowed the 25-pounder field gun to revert to its artillery role. It first saw action at Gazala in May 1942 and subsequently Churchill tanks armed with 6-pounders claimed the first Tiger in Tunisia. This particular gun is under fire to the south of El Alamein. (*Author's Collection*)

The American M3 medium tank had a tremendous impact, its firepower and numbers alone giving the Eighth Army some much-needed punch. The Grants were issued to the units of the 7th and 10th Armoured Divisions ready for the Battle of El Alamein. This particular tank is a General Lee undergoing crew training in America; American instructors and mechanics were also sent to Egypt. (*US Army/NARA*)

A British officer examines a smashed Panzer Mark IV 'Special'. The internal blast was so great that it has lifted the hull off the chassis; note the distinctive early, single-baffle, globular muzzle-brake on the L/43 gun. During the first Battle of El Alamein the Axis forces lost only half the number of tanks as the British but suffered twice the casualties. (*Author's Collection*)

An Axis supply train is strafed by a passing fighter. Initially the Luftwaffe largely dominated the skies over North Africa, but as the Desert Air Force gained experience and built up its strength its support for the ground war became relentless. As a prelude to Montgomery's offensive, Axis lines of communication, transport and supplies were attacked by fighters and medium bombers. (*Author's Collection*)

Montgomery has gone down in history as a rather cautious general. Certainly before El Alamein he ensured that he had enough tanks to deliver a knock-out blow. Even then Rommel gave him a run for his money, despite saying he had 'no hope' in the face of such numbers. (*Author's Collection*)

A troop of welded-hull M4A2 Shermans, having just refuelled, are poised for action. Armed with a 75mm gun, the Sherman first saw action at Alamein and was a reasonable match for the panzers in Egypt and Libya. (*Author's Collection*)

A British M3 Grant (distinguishable from the Lee by the lack of a commander's/machine-gun cupola on the turret) kicks up a dust storm in the Western Desert. The Grant was a welcome replacement for the inadequate British-designed Crusader tank and could not have arrived at a better time. (*Author's Collection*)

Although the Crusader III had increased armour and sported the 6-pounder gun, only 144 were built between May and July 1942. While the total output for the Crusader tank was an impressive 5,300 vehicles, German anti-tank guns never had any trouble picking them off in the desert fighting. (*Author's Collection*)

A British 4.5-inch field gun shelling enemy positions. This weapon had a good range, but the 5.5-inch gun which was coming into service could fire a shell twice the weight. The heavy British barrage on the night of 23 October 1942 signalled the start of the decisive second Battle of El Alamein. (*Author's Collection*)

In the opening stages of the attack, clearing paths through enemy minefields was a vital task if the Eighth Army's tank losses were to be kept to a minimum. These sappers had one of the most dangerous but essential tasks. (*Author's Collection*)

A Sikh from one of the Indian divisions escorts a prisoner of war past a knocked-out Panzer III. Between them is a 'Jerry' can; these proved invaluable for carrying both fuel and water – the German design ensured that it did not get crushed (unlike the earlier, thinner, containers). The open landscape behind them shows what good tank country this was. (*Author's Collection*)

A disabled Italian M13/40 or M14/41. The sandbags on the front of the hull were supposed to help supplement the tank's armour. While the M13 corrected many of the M11's faults, having the commander double-up as the gunner was not a desirable feature. Italian tanks remained under-gunned and under-armoured. (*Author's Collection*)

British infantry posing for the camera advance past a burning panzer. By 4 November 1942 Rommel had just twenty tanks left. (*Author's Collection*)

Another clearly posed shot portraying Australian infantry advancing through a smokescreen, following up behind the armour. (*Author's Collection*)

This familiar photograph shows Montgomery hitching a lift in a Sherman tank during the Battle of El Alamein. On the eve of his offensive he had 285 Shermans, although only 252 were listed on the Eighth Army's operational order of battle. (*NARA*)

The dead crew of a knocked-out German 50mm anti-tank gun are searched after their position was captured in the opening stages of the Eighth Army offensive. (*Author's Collection*)

Having been driven out of Egypt, Rommel's troops were forced to abandon much of their heavy equipment, such as this 15cm sFH 13/1 (sf) auf Geschützwagen Lorraine Schlepper (f) self-propelled gun. The object at the back of the hull is the recoil spade designed to brace the vehicle when firing. (*Australian Army*)

Another self-propelled gun lost by DAK. Sixty-six examples of this type of Czech/Russian hybrid known as the Marder were supplied to Rommel's troops. (*Australian Army*)

A captured Büssing Nag half-track prime mover which was used to tow German artillery. (*US Signal Corps/NARA*)

Once more posing for the camera, British infantry take cover behind the wrecked remains of a lorry during the Alamein battle. By this stage Rommel's remaining panzers were firmly on the run. (*Author's Collection*)

A Crusader III leads a column of Sherman M4A1s and Carriers through a liberated Mersa Matruh following the victory at El Alamein. Axis forces in the town tried to put up a fight but the Eighth Army skirted it and the garrison soon found themselves under attack from the east and the west. A souvenir of the battle in the shape of a German helmet can be seen lying on the hull of the Crusader. (*Author's Collection*)

The immediate culmination of Monty's victory at El Alamein, the Union Jack is once again hoisted over the port of Tobruk. Next stop, Tripoli. (*Author's Collection*)

Three British soldiers pose on top of a knocked-out Panzer III Ausf L or M (identifiable by the lack of turret side ports in front of the side hatches). The man in the middle appears to be clasping a tank round. (*Steve Hunnisett/Ron Hunnisett RA*)

Another knocked-out Panzer III. In the initial stages of the war in North Africa German mechanics were very efficient in retrieving battle casualties. Reporter Alexander Clifford noted, 'Lame tanks were dragged from the battle while the firing was still on, tended in a mobile workshop almost on the spot, and flung back into the fighting the next day. Our recovery units . . . simply were not organised like that.' At El Alamein Rommel lost almost all his panzers. (*Steve Hunnisett/Ron Hunnisett RA*)

A German officer overseeing a burial detachment. Rommel's losses were such that there would be no bouncing back, just a long fighting retreat. (*Dr Peter Caddick-Adams*)

Two German infantrymen take a meal-break in the midday sun. Having lost almost all his armour, Rommel was reliant on stoical infantry such as these men conducting a successful fighting retreat. (*Dr Peter Caddick-Adams*)

Chapter Ten

Kasserine – The Panzers' Last Hurrah

Just four days after Montgomery's breakthrough at El Alamein on 8 November 1942 the American Army landed in Vichy-controlled French Algeria and Morocco, west of Rommel in Libya. Due to a lack of tank-landing craft, the Moroccan ports of Casablanca and Safi on the Atlantic coast and the Algerian ports of Oran and Algiers on the Mediterranean had to be secured as quickly as possible in order for the Americans to land their tanks over the quayside.

There were around 50,000 French and colonial troops in Algeria and 55,000 in Morocco (with another 15,000 in Tunisia), supported by up to 500 aircraft. The French and French colonial forces were largely infantry formations, equipped with 25mm and 37mm anti-tank guns. However, according to American intelligence, they were supported by around 250 armoured cars and tanks, which constituted a direct threat to the American landing forces. Armour in French North Africa included the tiny Renault FT-17, Renault R-35 and Hotchkiss H-35/39 light tanks.

General Ernest H. Harmon, commanding the American landings, found he was without armour despite planned support from the American 1st and 2nd Armored Divisions. Those light tanks that had been landed were inoperable due to faulty batteries or drowned engines. To make matters worse, the two ships carrying additional tanks suffered critical delays unloading their cargo owing to crane problems. When the Shermans of Task Force Blackstone finally landed near Safi they were too late to see any combat. Task Force Goalpost, assigned to capture the airport at Lyautey and Sale, included M5 light tanks of the 66th Armored Regiment, 2nd Armored Division.

The 1st Armored Division comprised the 1st and 13th Armored Regiments, each equipped with one battalion of light tanks and two battalions of medium tanks. While the medium tanks were dry-landed at the portside, the light tanks were brought ashore via shallow-draft oil tankers and pontoon bridging. The M3 light tanks of the 13th Armored Reconnaissance Company, spearheading Red Task Force, seized Tafaraoui airfield. Green Task Force, including the M3s of the 1st Battalion plus elements of the 701st Tank Destroyer Battalion, secured La Senia airfield. Luckily the

American light tanks were more than a match for the elderly Renault tanks. It was only when the Sherman tanks were finally put ashore at Safi and Oran that the Allies were able to field any substantial quantity of medium armour, and by then the French had called for a ceasefire.

While elements of the US 2nd Armored Division took part in Operation Torch, only the US 1st Armored Division fought in Tunisia. Its sister division remained in French Morocco to help deter General Franco's Spain from joining the Axis powers. During the winter of 1942/43 the 2nd Armored Division was cannibalised to provide equipment for the newly raised French 2nd Armoured Division and to flesh out the 1st Armored Division after its mauling at Kasserine.

If the French had cooperated, the Allies could have pushed into Tunisia within two days of the landings in Algeria. Instead, the Germans struck westwards from Tunis, successfully safeguarding the panzers' escape from Libya into Tunisia. Under the French–Italian armistice, Mussolini had imposed a 50-mile demilitarised zone between Libya and Tunisia, but this now counted for nothing as German and Italian tanks were soon crossing to secure their exposed western flank. The French garrison in Tunisia chose to observe the ceasefire and join the Allies, as elements of the British First Army, after landing in eastern Algeria, moved into western Tunisia. Unfortunately, a quarter of the French garrison in Tunis remained loyal to Vichy France and did nothing to impede the arriving Germans. At Bizerte some Vichy French units even joined the Germans, who were moving to reinforce Tunisia.

The Allies' inability to extend the landings eastwards into Tunisia was to prove a major failing of Operation Torch. Within days of the Allied landings, German aircraft were flying troops and equipment into Tunis and by the end of the month some 15,000 German and 9,000 Italian troops were in position to prevent the British 1st Army from cutting through Tunisia to link up with the Eighth Army advancing through Libya.

In the wake of the Torch landings, the French had to support the Allies' forces in Tunisia, maintain their garrison forces and equip a new army to take part in the forthcoming liberation of Europe. This meant that ill-equipped existing units were rushed into battle before they were really combat ready. Initially the French 19 Corps, comprising some 13,000 men, moved to the front between the British 1st Army and the US 2 Corps. Crucially they lacked tanks. A similar number of Free French forces were also committed, and they were issued with Stuarts and Shermans.

Shortly after the German build-up in Tunisia, the Eighth Army rolled up to the Libyan border. During the second week of December Rommel decided to pull back from El Agheila, the Axis stop line during the two previous British advances. Instead, he chose to make a stand on the Mareth Line in Tunisia. Ironically this had been built by the French to keep the Italians out and was superior to the Alamein positions.

From Oran the US 1st Armored Division was rushed to Tunisia and came under the command of the British 1st Army for the drive on Tunis. The division's 2nd Battalion, 13th Armored Regiment, lost forty-two tanks to the panzers in fighting around Djedeiba and Tebourba. Despite receiving Sherman replacements, by the time of the Axis surrender the 1st Armored Division still had fifty-one M3s on its strength. These were handed over to the Free French forces for driver training. The M3 was then withdrawn from service in the Mediterranean and European theatres of operation.

By the end of January 1943 the Afrika Korps was in Tunisia, having abandoned Mussolini's Libyan colony with the evacuation of Tripoli. With his front secured on the Mareth Line, Rommel knew that he would be granted a breathing space by Montgomery that would enable him to turn and face the American Army advancing on Tunisia. Rommel kept hoping that Hitler would send him reinforcements, but when they arrived they were too few and too late.

Rommel's forces numbered about 30,000 Germans and 48,000 Italians. His 21st Panzer Division had been sent back to the Gabes-Sfax area, while the Italian Centauro Armoured Division had moved to guard the El Guettar defile facing the Americans at Gafsa. The German units, though, only had about one-third of their complement of tanks, a quarter of their anti-tank guns and a sixth of their artillery; of 130 panzers, less than half were combat-worthy.

Hitler, having starved Rommel of resources throughout 1941 and 1942, was now determined to hold on in Tunisia at all costs and by the beginning of February Axis forces had risen to a total of up to 100,000 Germans and an additional 26,000 Italians. The armoured forces were now almost entirely German and numbered 280 tanks, 110 with the 10th Panzer Division, ninety-one with the 21st Panzer Division, a dozen Tiger tanks and twenty-six tanks in a unit reinforcing the twenty-three surviving Italian tanks with the battered Centauro Division.

While Rommel was keen to strike before Montgomery gained the full benefit of the port of Tripoli, his chain of command was now complicated. His 21st Panzer Division was under General von Arnim's Tunisian command. At the end of January the 21st Panzer Division gained a foothold at the Faid Pass, from where it could launch an attack on the Americans. Rommel and von Arnim must have secretly despaired of fighting a two-front war in Tunisia. At last, having received fresh armoured units (which included the Herman Goering Division and the 501st Heavy Tank Battalion equipped with Tiger tanks), Rommel chose to set about the Americans at Kasserine. Only at Kasserine Pass did the exhausted Germans enjoy any real success against the inexperienced American tank crews pressing on their western flank.

On 14 February 1943 Rommel's veteran 21st and von Arnim's 10th Panzer Divisions swept through the American positions. The raw American troops were no match for the battle-hardened panzers. The 21st Panzer Division set about the US

1st Armored Division at Sidi Bouzid, destroying numbers of Grant, Lee and Sherman tanks with ease. To the embarrassment of the American Army, they lost 150 tanks and 1,600 men captured in the heavy fighting. The Germans rolled on through Kasserine and Sbeitla. A week later the Germans captured another twenty tanks, thirty armoured personnel carriers and a similar number of anti-tank guns. However, American losses were swiftly and easily replaced.

Kasserine gave Rommel his last victory in Africa, but his lack of resources and high command interference meant his tactical victory never developed into a strategic success. Shortly afterwards, Rommel flew to Berlin to request an evacuation, but not only did Hitler refuse this request, he also cruelly refused Rommel permission to return to his men, who were facing final defeat.

American troops embarking on transport ships bound for French North Africa. Operation Torch, launched on 8 November 1942, was designed to trap Rommel, who was being driven out of Egypt following El Alamein. (*US Army Signal Corps/NARA*)

A French gunboat moored at Casablanca. Despite putting out feelers, the Allies were unsure how the Vichy colonial armed forces would react to the landings in French Morocco and Algeria. (*Author's Collection*)

US troops in North Africa on 10 November 1942. Initially they had to rely on Stuart light tanks to provide armoured support against Vichy counter-attacks. (*US Army/NARA*)

Following the fall of France, quantities of equipment were hidden in North Africa, including half a dozen Hotchkiss tanks, such as these H-39s, twenty-five armoured cars and twenty-four tracked carriers. Additional tanks were then shipped from France to help counter the activities of the Free French. (*Author's Collection*)

Fortunately for the Americans, most Vichy counter-attacks involving tanks utilised the ancient two-man Renault FT-17. These were no match for the 1st Armored Division's M3 Stuarts, which moved to secure La Senia east of Oran. Between Lyautey and Rabat the 2nd Armored Division's M5 light tanks helped thwart thirty-two French tanks, forcing the crews to abandon twenty-four of them. (*Normandie Collection*)

General Eisenhower's inability to push his armoured units swiftly into Tunisia was to have serious ramifications. (*US Army/NARA*)

The French *Chasseurs d'Afrique* regiments were equipped with armoured cars and Renault R-35 tanks (as seen here) in North Africa. (*Author's Collection*)

In French West Africa armoured units were armed with twenty-three Somua S-35 tanks; after Operation Torch, they were shipped north to take part in the fighting against the Axis forces in Tunisia. (*Author's Collection*)

The 2nd Battalion, 13th Armored Regiment, 1st Armored Division, equipped with the M3 Grant/Lee, was the only medium tank battalion to take part in the initial landings in French North Africa. (*US Army/NARA*)

A 1st Armored Division M3 medium tank rumbles into Tunisia. The 2nd Battalion, 13th Armored Regiment, came under the British First Army for the drive on Tunis. They got to within 11 miles of their objective before mounting German resistance brought them to a halt. When the unit was pulled out of the line on 10 December 1942, it had just twelve tanks left; the other forty-two had been lost in the fighting around Djedeiba and Tebourba. (*US Army Signal Corps/NARA*)

The Germans moved swiftly to secure Rommel's rear by flying troops from Sicily into the key Tunisian towns of Bizerte, Gabes, Sfax and Tunis within days of Operation Torch. The Junkers Ju52 transport aircraft was instrumental in this airlift, but this air bridge came at a cost: on 18 April 1943 fifty-two aircraft from a force of about a hundred were shot down near Cape Bon. (*Scott Pick Collection & Dr Peter Caddick-Adams*)

Men of the American 601st Tank Destroyer Battalion pore over a map in front of the basic M2 half-track somewhere in Tunisia. Note the 75mm gun motor carriage M3 in the background. (*US Army/NARA*)

Members of the Headquarters Company, 2nd Battalion, 6th Armored Infantry Regiment, 1st Armored Division, scan the sky for enemy aircraft over Tunisia on 24 February 1943. (*US Army/NARA*)

The Focke Wulf Fw190 served in North Africa from late 1942 until the German collapse in Tunisia the following year. It made its combat debut on 16 November 1942, providing ground support; over Tunisia it engaged American, British and French aircraft with its pilots achieving a high number of kills. (*Author's Collection*)

Men of the 2nd Battalion, 16th Infantry Regiment, marching through the Kasserine Pass and on to Kasserine and Farriana on 26 February 1943. (*US Signal Corps/NARA*)

(*Above*) American GIs examining a knocked-out panzer; at first glance it looks like a Mk III, but the eight road wheels identify it as a Mk IV. (*US Signal Corps/NARA*)

(*Opposite, top*) The Tiger I deployed to North Africa in late 1942 with elements of the 501st Heavy Panzer Battalion; appropriately the unit's emblem was a stalking tiger. They were followed by a company of Tiger tanks from the 504th Heavy Tank Battalion in March 1943. (*US Signal Corps/NARA*)

(*Opposite, below*) US Army personnel inspect a captured M13/40. The Italians fought with great bravery to the last with their German allies in Tunisia. (*US Signal Corps/NARA*)

On the day of the Axis surrender in Tunisia, 12 May 1943, an American has stopped to look at smashed panzers on the roadside. The man is standing in front of the road wheels of a Tiger I, behind which is a Panzer IV. To the left is the hull of an upturned Tiger, while just in front of the speeding truck is another upturned Tiger. (*US Signal Corps/NARA*)

Judging by all the spent shells, this German 88mm gun gave a good account of itself defending Axis forces in Tunisia before it was knocked out by a Sherman. (*US Signal Corps/NARA*)

These GIs could not resist taking this captured and rebadged German hardware for a test drive. The tank on the left is a Panzer Mk II, while to the right they are examining a Sd Kfz 233 armoured car employed in the self-propelled gun role with a short 75mm gun. (*US Signal Corps/NARA*)

It's all over for these German prisoners as they file into a field near Bizerte on 8 May 1943 under the watchful eye of their American guards. (*US Signal Corps/NARA*)

This follow-up shot makes it apparent just how many men have laid down their arms. (*US Signal Corps/NARA*)

Chapter Eleven

Mareth and Longstop – The Road to Tunis

Montgomery was always able to trade hardware, a luxury that Rommel could ill afford. The Second Battle of Alamein was hard-won, but Monty's heavy tank losses were not fatal, whereas Rommel's were. By mid-January 1943 Montgomery could deploy 450 tanks against Rommel's thirty-six panzers and fifty-seven Italian tanks. The 7th Armoured Division's attack on the 15th Panzer Division on 15 January cost thirty-three tanks for just two panzers destroyed, and the following day the British lost another twenty tanks. The attack towards Tarhuna resulted in further severe losses for the British, but Rommel had nothing with which to hold on to Tripoli, which was captured on the 23rd.

Britain's armoured formations also enjoyed increasingly effective air support. By the time of the Second Battle of Alamein the Desert Air Force was able to fly on a daily basis some 2,500 fighter and fighter-bomber sorties and 800 bomber sorties. In contrast the Luftwaffe could only manage a hundred fighter sorties and sixty dive-bomber sorties in support of Rommel's beleaguered panzers.

Axis forces numbering 120,000 men with around 200 effective tanks were now facing over half a million Allied soldiers equipped with 1,800 tanks. Trying to capitalise on their success at Kasserine on 6 March 1943, a second Axis attack was mounted, this time against the Eighth Army opposite the Mareth Line towards Medenine. Up until late February Montgomery only had a single division at Medenine, but by the time of Rommel's attack he had quadrupled his strength there, with 400 tanks supported by 500 anti-tank guns and 350 field guns. Montgomery also had air superiority.

Rommel's three panzer divisions could muster only 160 tanks supported by no more than 10,000 infantry and 200 guns. It was an ill-executed operation and was repulsed with heavy losses, including fifty precious tanks, in the face of overwhelming British firepower. Although the 15th Panzer Division closed on the enemy, it was driven off. The 21st Panzer Division, which should have known better, exposed its tanks crossing a ridge; they took a terrible beating and were never able to close on the British gun lines. Neither the 10th Panzer Division nor the 90th Light Division achieved any better results and all suffered from mines. The British did not lose a single tank and only suffered minimal casualties – how times had changed.

As the Afrika Korps withdrew, it could only muster eighty-five German and twenty-four Italian tanks, a dangerously low number with which to hold on to Tunisia. On 9 March Rommel took his long-deferred sick leave and handed over the command of the army group to von Arnim. Rommel's Panzerarmee Afrika now became known as the 1st Italian Army under General Giovanni Messe; against it, Montgomery had a 4:1 superiority in tanks.

On 20 March Montgomery threw 610 tanks at the Mareth Line, which was defended by just 150 tanks. However, his assault was driven off thanks to the weather, which kept the RAF grounded, and the panzers' determination. The main defences of the Mareth Line ran along the formidable natural barrier of the Wadi Zigzaou, which after bitter fighting was forced by elements of the British 50th Division. A well-timed counter-attack by the 15th Panzer Division with less than thirty tanks and two infantry battalions contained and then almost destroyed the British bridgehead.

This forced Montgomery to redeploy the 1st Armoured Division to the west to support the New Zealand Corps' left hook towards El Hamma. The New Zealanders barged through Wilder's Gap in the Matmata Hills and across the waterless Dahar to the Tebaga Gap behind the Afrika Korps' flank, forcing them to withdraw from the Mareth Line. Nonetheless, the blocking forces of the 21st Panzer Division at El Hamma ensured that the Axis forces were not trapped, though the panzer divisions lost most of their tanks during the battle.

Montgomery then launched a frontal assault on the new Axis position at Wadi Akarit, which spanned the Gabes Gap, forcing a breach. General Messe, with the Americans bearing down on his right flank, withdrew north toward Enfidaville. Slowly but surely the Axis forces were trapped in northern Tunisia around the ports of Bizerte and Tunis by the American and British armies.

With the Eighth Army pushing up from the south, the 1st Army began an offensive from the west. The key armoured formations were the US 1st Armored and the British 1st, 6th and 7th Armoured Divisions. Still the Axis forces clung to their mountain defences, especially on Longstop Hill where the British 78th Division struggled for four days to retake control from the Germans. In late April the panzers of the Afrika Korps made one last attack in an attempt to stave off the inevitable. General von Arnim gathered all the remaining armoured detachments into the 8th Panzer Regiment, which had first fought during Operation Battleaxe, and counter-attacked at Djebel Bou Aoukaz west of Longstop. The Afrika Korps had just sixty-nine panzers still fit for battle, save for one very important detail – petrol.

During early May Allied forces began to encroach onto the Tunisian coastal plain. On the 5th the British 1st Infantry Division took Djebel Bou Aoukaz and the next day the 4th Indian Division secured the Medjez el Bab position. The way was now open for the 'Desert Rats' of the 7th Armoured Division and on 7 May their tanks rolled triumphantly into Tunis. At the same time the Americans took Bizerte, leaving the remaining Axis forces trapped in the Cape Bon peninsula.

On 12 May 1943 von Arnim himself was captured and a day later Messe formally surrendered 125,000 German and 115,000 Italian troops, all of whom went into captivity. The Axis forces' remaining 250 immobile tanks fell into the Allies' hands. On the 13th General Alexander signalled Churchill in London, 'Sir, it is my duty to report that the campaign in Tunisia is over. All enemy resistance has ceased. We are masters of the North African shores.'

New Zealand infantry charge through the smoke to overrun an enemy position during the Wadi Matratin operation to outflank Rommel at El Agheila. Following Rommel's defeat at El Alamein, the Eighth Army rolled back into Mersa Matruh, Sidi Barrani, Bardia, Tobruk and Benghazi. The New Zealanders' carriers then left-hooked again to Nofilia, but the lack of tank support meant the German rearguard held. (*Author's Collection*)

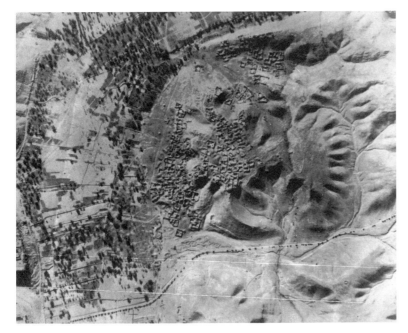

Axis motor vehicles streamed westward through Tripolitania towards Tunisia: the 'dotted line' towards the bottom of the frame is a convoy heading through the wadis near Bendi Ulid. Bumper to bumper, they were vulnerable to air attack. (*Author's Collection*)

British forces rolled into the port of Tripoli at 5am on 23 January 1943. This photo clearly shows Eighth Army Valentine tanks and tracked carriers in the central square. In the foreground are Ford 3-ton trucks, with what appears to be the CMP cab No. 12 known as the 'Alligator' hood. (*Author's Collection*)

A British soldier surveys the view from a Mareth
Line outpost just outside Foum Tatanouine, which
dominates several approach roads. Although
trenches were cut in the rock to connect a
number of concrete pillboxes, it is clear from the
fact that this man is kneeling that these were little
more than temporary defensive positions for light
weapons. (*Author's Collection*)

In January 1943, following El Alamein, Montgomery
could still field 450 tanks; the following month he
attacked the Mareth Line with over 600. Against
such numbers there was little Rommel could do
but continue his fighting retreat, and Monty's
habitual caution ensured that Rommel kept getting
away. (*Author's Collection*)

Tired-looking men of the Eighth Army negotiate an Axis anti-tank ditch on the Mareth Line. The New Zealanders turned the Matmata Hills by driving west through Wilder's Gap, opening up a left hook to Bir Soltane and ultimately El Hamma. The loss of the Mareth position cost Rommel 6,000 men captured as well as quantities of panzers, transport vehicles and other equipment lost, but he still managed to get away with the bulk of his forces. (*Author's Collection*)

Churning up the sand, a British Crusader II close support tank, armed with a 3-inch howitzer, leads two Crusader IIIs (identifiable by the flat gun mantlet and 6-pounder gun) through the town of El Hamma. While this move unhinged the Mareth Line, the actions of the veteran 21st Panzer Division enabled Rommel to fall back on Gabes and then Wadi Akarit, ensuring that he escaped Montgomery once again. (*Author's Collection*)

(*Above*) Kicking up the dust, a British Grant tank pushes through Gabes hot on the heels of the Italian Saharan Group and the German 21st Panzer and 164th Light Divisions, which screened the Axis retreat from Mareth. (*Author's Collection*)

(*Opposite, top*) A column of Valentine tanks waiting patiently while sappers mark out a mine-free route on the approaches to the Gabes Gap. Just 10 miles north of El Hamma and Gabes, Rommel turned to fight at Wadi Akarit, which spans the gap (a narrow-fronted position between the Mediterranean and the nearby hills). Earlier American attempts to secure this position had failed. This enabled Rommel to fight a successful two-front battle against the British and the Americans. (*Author's Collection*)

(*Opposite, below*) Valentine tanks, carriers and motor transport vehicles take a break after pushing through the Gabes Gap. Note the prisoners of war moving off to the left. (*Author's Collection*)

(*Above*) An Eighth Army welded-hull Sherman M4A2 takes a slight detour while sappers using a bulldozer repair a road blown up by the retreating Axis forces. Note the rather random camouflage scheme. This photo was taken during the push on Wadi Akarit. (*Author's Collection*)

(*Opposite, top*) British troops check out a knocked-out panzer in Tunisia. Sightseers often had to be careful of booby traps left by fleeing crews. (*Author's Collection*)

(*Opposite, below*) The Bishop was the first British-designed self-propelled gun of the war, and consisted of a Valentine chassis with a 25-pounder gun in a fixed turret. Supplied in limited numbers to the Eighth Army, it was soon eclipsed by the M7 Priest using the M3 medium tank chassis. The Bishop was crude and unsophisticated by comparison. Dubbed 'a formidable combination', these three are firing near Grenadier Hill in Tunisia. (*Author's Collection*)

Churchill tanks providing infantry support near Longstop Hill. It was planned to halt production of this tank in 1943, but its first real combat operations with the First Army in the Tunisian hills gained it a reprieve. It was usually armed with a 6-pounder gun, but some of the First Army's tanks were up-gunned with the M3's 75mm gun to produce the Churchill IV (NA 75). (*Author's Collection*)

A Tiger I knocked out in Tunisia. The British first came up against Hitler's latest and heaviest tank near Pont du Fahs in February 1943 when 6-pounder anti-tank guns took on nine Panzer IIIs and two Tigers. Both the Tigers were knocked out at 500 yards. (*US Signal Corps/NARA*)

The British First Army entered Tunis in the late afternoon of 7 May 1943 and the men were greeted as liberators by the locals. Shermans such as this one were brought up to silence any lingering resistance from enemy snipers. (*Author's Collection*)

While Luftwaffe personnel in North Africa escaped to Sicily, much of their equipment was not so fortunate. Here a British soldier at Bizerte aerodrome is examining an abandoned Focke Wulf which was damaged in an Allied bombing raid. (*Author's Collection*)

A column of German prisoners captured outside Bizerte on 8 May 1943. Many of them look almost relieved that it is all over. (*US Signal Corps/NARA*)

The Axis forces ended up with some strange bedfellows in Tunisia. The tricolour on the man's helmet shows that these are members of the French Phalange Africaine, who were attached to the German 334th Infantry Division. When the 5th Panzer Army surrendered, it included five battalions of locally raised Arabs. (*Author's Collection*)

Bedraggled-looking German prisoners captured at Medjez el Bab. They appear to have abandoned all their personal equipment except their greatcoats. The men on the right are wearing the long canvas and leather desert boots popular with the Deutsches Afrika Korps. Again they seem relieved the fighting is over and that they are alive. (*Author's Collection*)

General Harold Alexander in Tunisia. On 13 May 1943 he signalled Churchill, 'We are masters of the North African shores.' (*Author's Collection*)

The final resting place of many Panzertruppen in Tunisia. Hitler's insistence on fighting to the bitter end in North Africa greatly depressed Rommel, who saw little point in such futile gestures. While the 15th and 21st Panzer Divisions were reformed in Sicily and Normandy respectively, they had to be fleshed out with new recruits. (*US Signal Corps/NARA*)

The very last of the panzers disabled by Allied bombers. This Panzer Mk IV was photographed on 10 May 1943, just days before the Axis surrender. The force of the explosion blew the turret hatch and the engine grill clean off. (*US Signal Corps/NARA*)

American Sherman M4A2s gathered at La Pecherie French naval base in Tunisia in July 1943 ready for the next major military operation in the Mediterranean: the invasion of Sicily. (*US Army/NARA*)

A veteran of the North African battles comes ashore in Sicily. (*US Army/NARA*)

Following the German surrender in Tunisia in May 1943, British Shermans were next deployed in the invasion of Sicily – this one is north of Rammacca. Subsequently 1,600 Shermans were delivered to the Eighth Army in Italy. (*Author's Collection*)